OF STRANGERS & ENEMIES

J ROBERT EAGAN

OF STRANGERS & ENEMIES

A Pathway to Peace for Jews, Christians, & Muslims

J Robert Eagan

Copyright © 2016 J Robert Eagan

All rights reserved.

ISBN: 0692652159

ISBN-13: 978-0692652152

Library of Congress Control Number: 2016903275

Cover Design: Dave Crow

To my wife, who inspired the rhetoric that became the focus of this book and who patiently sat next to me and stood by me in the process of making this work a reality.

Contents

Acknowledgments

Special thanks to all of my friends and family who helped make this project become a reality, whether through edits and commentary or financial gifts. I couldn't have done this without you. Thanks to Josh Berardi and Bassel Riche for taking extra time to give detailed feedback on the first draft and to Misty Dykema, Josh Graber, Ted Rice and my mom for helping me make this book more accessible to a broader audience. Thanks to Kevin Bushnell and Annette Fudge for giving critical feedback on the final draft.

Landon, thanks for letting me crash on your couch for a month while I finished the first draft. Thanks to Ty, John, Eric, and Neelam for living this out in your lives. Thanks to the faculty of Fuller Theological Seminary for helping me to learn to write and think well. Thanks to Catherine Orsborn for always being willing to promote the work that I am doing to create spaces for peace to break out in our communities. Thanks to my wife for being brave, for being patient, and for choosing to walk alongside me as we work together to live the words I have written. And thanks be to God, who is working to bring about the reconciliation of all humankind.

We have reason to hope for a better future.

Introduction

I started a love revolution at the San Antonio airport in my mind.

I woke up at 4:00 a.m. and headed to the airport to fly home after a long weekend. I was in San Antonio primarily to teach a group of Christian college students about Islam and to encourage them to engage in meaningful and transformative relationships with Muslims they know. I also spent an extensive amount of time in conversations with others I work with about love, peace, and government. It made for a pretty long weekend.

When I got to my gate, I realized I was at least an hour early for my flight, which is not a great realization at 5:40 a.m. I had nothing to do, and I was overtired. I noticed a guy rehearsing something from a typed piece of paper, over and over again, sitting about ten feet away from me. He seemed to be nervous about whatever it was. He kept mouthing the words, getting stuck, looking back at the paper, and getting frustrated with himself for not having the whole thing down pat. Seeing this kicked off a conversation between my head and my heart that went something like this.

My heart said, "You should help that guy."

My head said, "No, I'm tired and I will probably just offend him or something."

My heart said, "Shut up, head! Let him try."

My head said, "You're too tired for an awkward interaction."

My head and my heart went back and forth for about a half hour.

I imagined myself going over to this guy and saying something like, "Hey, I noticed you seem to be trying to memorize whatever is on that sheet. Would it be helpful to practice with me? I mean, maybe if you had a real person to talk to, you wouldn't have to keep second-guessing yourself." I wanted to assure him that he was going to do awesome in his interview or tryout or oral exam or whatever. He was obsessing over an eventual doom scenario that might occur whenever he landed, and I wanted to help him out. In my imaginary scenario, he took me up on the offer and realized that he really was prepared. He realized he didn't have anything to worry about. Then people started listening to him and cheered for him when he absolutely nailed it. I got caught up in the fanfare of it all, equal parts proud of him and of myself for taking the risk and listening to my heart.

But, in reality, I just sat there and glanced at him every once in a while. Everything stayed just as it was—status quo.

After my imaginary tutoring was finished, I noticed a group of kids, all barely eighteen years old, dressed in camouflage and carrying backpacks. Some of them were sitting in close proximity to one another, and it looked as if they were heading to boot camp. Some were wearing headphones, while others were talking. I could sense the buzz of excitement among these young recruits as they were heading into the great unknown that we call the future. I wanted to talk with them about their lives and why they were heading off to boot camp. I wanted to know where they were from and what they hoped they would gain by joining the military—not to be contrarian or difficult but to learn their stories.

Not too long after that, a small girl with flushed cheeks walked into the waiting area, also in camouflage. She looked at the others and seemingly wanted to sit near them, but instead she timidly sat in a row by herself. She seemed very self-conscious and aware that she might not be as cool as the others heading off to war. I know that she was at least eighteen, but I seriously couldn't fathom that she was more than twelve years old. She was just a kid, and I couldn't believe that kids this young enlisted in the military. I imagined myself moving over to sit next to her and quickly began to create another scenario in my mind of how this interaction would play out. I asked her about where she was from, where she was headed, and why she was joining the military. I could sense her shyness melting away and a wash of comfort and belonging falling over her. She told me about her dad and how he had served in the first Gulf War. She said she was so proud of him for the way he had served his country and that he had inspired her journey to enlisting. She told me her mom didn't want her to enlist but also knew that this was the only way she would be able to go to college. She hadn't been such a good student.

But I just sat there.

I then watched as an old man took a seat next to her. He did exactly what I was wasting my time imagining myself doing—he engaged her in a conversation. She lit up like a child telling her parents about how she got almost all of the answers correct on her timed test in school. When boarding started, she was not with the others; she was flying to a different airport in a different state. I wondered if that was why she didn't join the other recruits. Perhaps she wasn't shy or self-conscious at all. Perhaps she just realized they weren't going where she was headed. Her future was somewhere else. She stood with the old man in line as if he were her grandpa, looking at him, listening, and smiling. I was proud of that man. I should have been that man.

Instead, I was just a part of the scenery. I let the world continue to be the disconnected place that it was. I let the world be just as harsh and lonely as it was. I did nothing to change that. I often say that you can't love what you fear. It's true. It was true that day in the airport. I was afraid of rejection, of being strange, of overstepping the boundaries that we erect between us in places like that. I talked myself out of the very love revolution that I wanted to be a part of every day and that I could have participated in had I not been so afraid of strangers.

What I realized that morning in San Antonio was that I talk a big game, but when it comes down to it, I have as many barriers and excuses as everyone else not to engage in conversations with my neighbors, strangers, or my enemies. I have grown accustomed to the status quo. And our status quo in America is really lonely and disconnected. It's terrible, and I could have done something about it.

If I could go back and relive that morning, I would say to the guy rehearsing for whatever he was rehearsing for, "I'm sorry, and I know you'll do a great job." Even more, I wish I could say to the little kids going off to war, "I hope that you never lose touch with your truest selves, the parts of you that compel you to love others and desire peace. Don't let your journey harden the goodness within you."

I share this story here not because I am proud of it, but because it's my reality. In the pages that follow, I have written some challenging and true things about what it means to love our neighbors, strangers, and our enemies. However, that does not mean I am living in some elevated state of consciousness in which I am always making the loving choice and living lovingly toward all people. My day-to-day reality consists of a lot of battles between my head and my heart. I want to live in a way that makes neighbors out of strangers and enemies, but I talk myself out of it most of the time.

I am thankful that in many ways, as a result of writing this book, I have fewer days in which my head wins the argument.

The first step toward changing the narrative of fear and isolation is to recognize that we are all a part of the problem. No one is immune to feeling less than adequate. No one is immune to the fear of rejection or, worse, of saying the wrong thing and offending someone. However, I think we all, in some way, intuitively know that in order for anything to change, we have to step out of our isolation and into engagement with the proverbial "other." It's one thing to imagine doing that in the airport. It's another to imagine doing that across lines of religious difference. But there is no area of greater need and no more relevant time than this to start the process of peace through first imagining and then engaging in relationships across those very lines of religious or cultural difference. This is my invitation for you to join me in crafting a better future for all of us.

Who and Why?

My friend Jared asked me why I was focusing my writing and my work on only Jews, Christians, and Muslims. After all, there are many religions in the world and they all have something to say about peace. This is true. Buddhists and Hindus, in particular, are some of the most peaceful people on the planet. No doubt, those religious systems have much to offer when it comes to learning how to live at peace with one another, though they too are not immune to extremism in their ranks. So what is so significant about these three religions that I have chosen to write a book exploring how they teach their followers how to love neighbors, strangers, and enemies?

Jews, Christians, and Muslims all trace their religious heritage to Abraham. Jews are descendants of Isaac (Abraham's second child); Muslims, particularly Arab Muslims, are descendants of Ishmael (Abraham's first child); and Christians see themselves as grafted into the family of Abraham through Jesus Christ. Basic, if not core, to all three Abrahamic faiths is the understanding that we are to love our neighbors. For Muslims, Jews, and Christians, this also presents a problem. How do we make sense of the command to love our neighbors when we naturally isolate ourselves from one another? How are we to make sense of the command to love the stranger as ourselves when we have made strangers of everyone around us? How does the command to love our enemies play out when we would much rather ignore or, worse, demonize them?

More than half the world's population is contained within these three Abrahamic faiths, which makes these questions even more important. Prince Ghazi bin Muhammad of Jordan has suggested that for any hope of meaningful peace to be seen in our time, Muslims and Christians need to be living at peace.[1] I believe that beyond these two religions, we need to also consider how Judaism plays a role, not

---

[1] Miroslav Volf, Ghazi bin Muhammad, and Melissa Yarrington, eds., *A Common Word: Muslims and Christians on Loving God and Neighbor* (Grand Rapids: William B. Eerdmans Pub. Co., 2010), 49.

only in having laid the foundation of Islam and Christianity, but also because of how important Israel remains to be in any conversation regarding peace in the Middle East. Muslims, Jews, and Christians are notoriously enemies of one another, despite the fact that we share so much in common—from a belief in one God and the desire for weighty and lasting peace (*shalom* or *salaam*) to the priority of loving our neighbors. The question we will seek to answer through the course of this book is this: How can we become neighbors toward and make neighbors out of strangers and enemies and then take steps on the pathway of peace—in our neighborhoods, cities, countries, and world?

What you will discover in the pages ahead is nothing new. Many books have been written in an attempt to help us understand these issues and to find a meaningful way toward peace among members of these three religions. However, much of that discussion takes place in the realm of academia. The reality is that many *normal* people either don't have access to or won't attempt to access those resources. For this reason, I felt it was important to distill some of this information in a way that a person who has never thought about these ideas can come to an understanding of them, as well as to inspire people from all backgrounds to see their lives as an important part of this peacemaking process.

My target audience has always been Christians from a variety of backgrounds. I have written this book with this particular group in mind. That is not to say that someone who is of Muslim or Jewish faith won't find meaning and purpose in these pages. Even more, a person from the outside looking in, either from another religious perspective or even from no religious perspective, will find hope and understanding in what follows. The goal from the start has been to encourage all people to begin to engage in relationships with people who believe differently than they do, because it is my belief that through relationships across lines of difference, we create spaces in our communities, our nations, and our world for peace to become a possibility.

Orientation

The first chapter is my story and more particularly, how a friendship transformed the way I understand my faith in a multifaith world. My story may resonate deeply with some readers, and others may find it to be rather odd. Regardless, if you don't understand what made me who I am today, you likely won't be able to understand why I care so deeply about this conversation. Chapters 2 to 5 are a survey of Judaism, Christianity, and Islam in regards to how each religion's text and traditions have informed the way Jews, Christians, and Muslims either can or should interact with their neighbors, strangers, and enemies. I have put my best effort into understanding each perspective on its own while also being as generous as possible, particularly when it comes to my understanding of Judaism and Islam. As an outsider looking in, my goal in these chapters has been to imagine what it might look like if we all lived according to the best our religions have to offer.

The final chapter is a prescription for peace that I have called dialogical friendships. What I am not talking about when I talk about dialogical friendships is *tolerance*. Tolerance is an urban virtue. Tolerance says, "Look! I have Muslim friends, and I have Jewish friends. We all get along just fine. All we have to do is avoid talking about our differences. We're all pretty much the same anyway." The problem with tolerance is precisely *that* it ignores differences and calls that friendship. If I can't talk with my friends about the most meaningful things in my life, then they don't really know me. As Dr. Martin Luther King Jr. said, "People fail to get along because they fear each other; they fear each other because they don't know each other; they don't know each other because they have not communicated with each other."[2] A dialogical friendship, as outlined in the final chapter, is one that encourages true communication across lines of difference. If we engage in our differences while seeking understanding, it will go a long way toward healing the divides between Jews, Christians, and Muslims. The reader will find some brief interludes between chapters. These are some additional thoughts based upon various topics and personal experiences that can help the reader think about what it means to love one's neighbors, strangers, and one's enemies and to seek peace in a multifaith world. Altogether, as I have stated, the goal is to find a way to make neighbors (or friends) out of strangers and enemies in order to make a way for peace to become a reality in our time.

---

[2] Martin Luther King, Jr., "Advice for Living," *Ebony*, May 1958, 401.

A Prayer

As this is a book about religions, about love, and about peace, I think it makes sense to offer this prayer, a prayer of St. Francis of Assisi, to guide our way forward. Feel free to refer back to this prayer as often as necessary to remind yourself of who you are in the world.

[God], make us instruments of your peace.
Where there is hatred, let us sow love;
Where there is injury, pardon;
Where there is discord, union;
Where there is doubt, faith;
Where there is despair, hope;
Where there is darkness, light;
Where there is sadness, joy.
Grant that we may not so much seek to be consoled as to console;
To be understood as to understand;
To be loved as to love.
For it is in giving that we receive;
It is in pardoning that we are pardoned;
And it is in dying that we are born to eternal life.
Amen.[3]

---

[3] "A Prayer Attributed to St. Francis," *Episcopal Book of Common Prayer*, 833.

1
A Story about How My Life
Got Turned Upside Down

Pekin to Phoenix: Miseducation

I am from Pekin. Pekin is a medium-sized town smack dab in the middle of Illinois. My town, where I lived for the first eighteen years of my life, was monochromatic. I looked just like everybody else. Everyone in Pekin was white, and almost everyone was some sort of Christian—Catholic, Lutheran, Methodist, Presbyterian, Episcopalian, Baptist, Pentecostal, or some other variation. We actually divided ourselves on these lines since we didn't have racial lines to distinguish us from others. That's what we do when surrounded by people who look the same; we have to find some way to label them. We have to know who is in and who is out. It's human nature.

I was raised Baptist, and we notoriously believed that Catholics were going to hell. We were pretty sure all of the other types of Christians were too. For instance, the girl who grew up in the house behind mine was, without my knowledge, a Christian. I met her later in life at a gathering of youth ministry people. She was the youth pastor at her church. I had thought she was going to hell (not when I met her later, but when we were growing up).

My high school had a student population of about 2,300 students. Of those students, 2,298 give or take, were white. Prior to 1981, our school mascot was the Chinks. In the 1970s, a delegation from a Chinese organization came to Pekin to ask us to change our offensive mascot to something else. The student body denied their request. When I was in high school, we became the Dragons (our backward way of still poking at the Chinese people and culture), and our school chant at sporting events was equally as racist: "P-P-P-E-K, *K-K-K*-I-N, P-E-K-K-I-N, Pekin, Pekin, Pekin!" We didn't know any better. After all, 2,298 of us found no personal offense in such a chant. You might think the K-K-K chant was simply a coincidence, except for the fact that the Ku Klux Klan actually owned and ran the Pekin newspaper in the 1920s. In 1949, the author of the *Pekin Centenary*, a book about Pekin's first century as a township, wrote the following:

> Pekin, for years unique because of its clinging to the old German ways, had so changed that it was soon to be unique in that no firm line was to exist between its people on any ground. *It was and remains unique, too, in the fact that there are no members of the colored race living in the city.* Apparently, the militancy of the early secessionist Knights of the Golden Circle (KKK), together with the long period when at least an understanding of German was essential to even moderate success in the community, combined to discourage any early settlement by colored people, and they have simply never become established here.[4]

Clearly, Pekin's heritage had discouraged diversity from becoming a public fact. Because of this, I didn't have much of an opportunity to interact with other cultures, except through books. I devoured books about my heroes Martin Luther King Jr. and Jackie Robinson.

---

[4] Thomas H. Harris, *The Pekin Centenary: 1849–1949* (Pekin: Pekin Association of Commerce, 1949), 57.

Something about these two captured my fascination, and despite my cultural situation, they caused me to think in different ways about race and culture than many of my friends.

The Baptist church I was raised in was strongly evangelistic. We believed that we had a corner on truth and the gospel, and we were taught ways in which we could convince others that they were going to hell when they died unless they believed the particular truth and gospel that we knew. Evangelism was all about learning the right techniques in order to maximize the results. And life was all about believing the right things in order to guarantee a place in heaven after death. So, we learned a simplified version of the gospel that demonstrated that no matter how good a person is, his or her ultimate destiny is hell unless he or she believes the correct things about Jesus.

Back then, evangelism was simple. Imagine a canyon. Let's say the Grand Canyon. On one side of the canyon, we have humanity, and on the other side of the canyon stands God. There is no way for humans to make their way to God, since at the bottom of this canyon is fire (as opposed to the Colorado River). That fire represents hell, which is eternal conscious torment forever and ever. Without help, every single human is separated from God and every effort people make to reach God will end with getting burned. Life is truly hopeless, no matter how good you are. But Jesus, who is God's Son, came to earth in order to die on a cross for our sins and that cross has become a bridge that crosses the great divide between humans and

God. All we have to do is believe the bridge story in order to make our way to God, which also means we avoid hell and get to spend eternity in heaven. This understanding of evangelism and the purpose of the gospel unfortunately served to reinforce the already ingrained act of *othering* I had learned from the culture of my community. Some people were in, but most were out.[5]

In my first year of Bible college, some friends and I made up a ministry (so we didn't necessarily have to serve in the church) that involved going to Arizona State University on Fridays and eating lunch with people. We were armed with questions and a desire to get out of the Christian bubble we were suffocating in on our own campus. On our first trip, I met Omar and Zach. Omar was Muslim, and Zach was agnostic about almost everything. We talked about peace and our life stories together. Omar's family was from somewhere in the non-Arabic-speaking Muslim world. I didn't have a framework in my mind for Islam or what it meant to be a Muslim, so I was curious. One Friday, Omar invited my friend and me to come to his class on world religions to watch the movie *The Matrix*. We weren't allowed to watch R-rated movies at my school, but we decided we could do so for the sake of "ministry."

That night, the teacher walked in and immediately apologized. She had left the DVD at home. Class was cancelled, and I was distraught. I really wanted to watch that movie (despite having seen

---

[5] This framework would be challenged later for me through interactions with amazing people from Catholic and other religious/denominational backgrounds.

it four or five times in the past). Instead, we headed to Subway to get a bite to eat. I decided to ask Omar about his faith. He said, "I read the Qur'an and pray every day. But I don't understand a word of it. I don't understand the language." I didn't know what to do with that information. My experience of Christianity had always been in my native tongue, and I didn't understand why his couldn't be. I didn't have any idea how to respond to this whatsoever, so I changed the subject. That was the last conversation I had with Omar. I simply quit my Friday visits to Arizona State altogether. I was afraid of his faith or perhaps my lack of ability to relate to his experience of it.

When I was back home in 2001, there was a guest speaker at my Baptist church one Sunday. He was incredibly concerned with the events that we all experienced on September 11. He spoke about how Islam was a demonic religion. I didn't have a visceral response to his words, and given the fact that my (former) friend Omar was a Muslim who read a book in a foreign language that he couldn't understand, I thought it might be the case. I didn't have any reason to object to his assertions at that point in my life, aside from the fact that his delivery made me incredibly uncomfortable. He was angry, and it showed.

During the second war in Iraq, I lived with my friends at a house in Phoenix, Arizona. I remember feeling relieved as I watched the news showing Saddam Hussein's statue being lassoed and pulled to the ground. Saddam was my boogeyman growing up; I remember hiding on the side of my waterbed (I would have been under it, but there was no "under") during the first Gulf War because I was afraid that the terrorists were going to get me. Saddam was the face of terrorism in the lives of many like me in the 1990s, and I was glad that the boogeyman was finally out of power. It all felt strangely personal to me. I didn't think about the people in Iraq who were actually being invaded by US forces. All I knew was that one more bad guy was out of power, and that *had* to be a good thing.

My friend Joey had traveled to Malaysia for a mission trip previously that year, and as a souvenir, he brought back an Arabic Qur'an that he had stolen from his hotel room. Being Bible college students with a penchant for backward humor and controversy, we decided it would be funny to put the Qur'an on a stand on the bookshelf in the entry of our house. For about a week, glass randomly broke in our house. Joey himself was holding a hand mirror (for no good reason), and the mirror just fell right out of it onto the tile floor in the kitchen. We were all utterly spooked. As Christians, we didn't believe in ghosts. We did, however, believe in demons. And given our small amount of experience, we attributed the occurrences to the open Arabic Qur'an on the bookshelf. We promptly closed the Qur'an and put it away, and glass stopped breaking—proof, we thought, that Islam was a demonic religion. After all, what other explanation could there be?

Getting Schooled

Everything began to change one fateful Friday night. My wife and I would routinely contact my parents on the weekend to get a free meal at a restaurant. We weren't coy about this—it was our modus operandi. So, just like every week prior to the one in question, I called up my parents to see what they were doing for dinner. My mom said, "We would love to do dinner with you guys, but we have a missionary staying with us, so we will all be going together." I told her I would have to call her back.

See, growing up in the church, I had many interactions with missionaries, none of which were life-giving experiences. I experienced missionaries to be condescending. Often they made me feel as if I wasn't truly living out my faith unless I was doing so in a foreign country, trying to save the souls of the lost people throughout the world.[6] I wasn't interested in that sort of an experience again. However, my stomach overruled my head, and I called my mom back to say that we would meet them at their place.

Rick wasn't like all of the other missionaries I knew. He was funny and kind and was reading some of the same books I was reading. Most important, he didn't condescend to me or make me feel like I was less faithful because I wasn't following his path. He also had a strange job as the pastor of an international church in Jordan. He wasn't working with Muslims but with Christians. Rick told me that the church was looking for a new youth pastor. Having gone to

---

[6] Not all missionaries are like this, but this was my experience prior to meeting Rick. I met many wonderfully loving missionaries in Jordan and continue to meet great people who are doing great things throughout the world. That being said, if you have had the same sort of experiences, you're not alone.

Bible college and having done youth ministry for several years, I impulsively said, "I'll be your youth pastor." I quickly glanced over at my wife, who shrugged and nodded in agreement.

Rick said, "Are you serious?"

I said, "Yeah, I think so."

Over the next several months, we started planning for our journey to the Middle East. We put our house on the market, got our passports, and began the process of interacting with the leaders of Rick's church. Through those conversations, however, we mutually decided that I was not a good fit for the church and that the church was not a good fit for us. We were incredibly disappointed. We *knew* that we were going to be moving to Jordan. We had put our future on hold for this potential adventure, and now we didn't know what to do.

As we researched ways that we could get out of Pekin and explore the world, I sent an e-mail to Rick to ask if there was anything we could do as volunteers for a semester in Jordan. He responded in the affirmative; we could work at an Iraqi refugee clinic run by his wife, we could volunteer teaching English at an English center in downtown Amman, and we could study Arabic. This sounded good to us, so we sold our house and moved to the Middle East. We didn't move because we wanted to save the world. We didn't move because we wanted to rescue Muslims from the clutches of their demonic religion. We didn't move there for any purpose except to do some good and to feel good about ourselves and return after four months for me to pursue a master's in theology. As crazy as it sounds in retrospect, it was simply a trip.

I took with me only what I had learned about Islam in the past. I knew that Muslims didn't like Jews and that Islam very well might be a demonic religion. In other words, I didn't know anything at all. I didn't spend any time researching Islam aside from reading the introduction to the Penguin Classics Qur'an that I had purchased prior to the trip. My Arabic language learning preceding the trip consisted solely of learning how to ask a person if he or she spoke English. I wasn't intentionally ethnocentric, but I really did think that was all I would need to know in order to get around. I had heard that most people spoke some amount of English in Jordan, so that was all the Arabic I should need. And suddenly, two white Christian kids from a medium-sized racist town in the middle of Illinois settled into a strange, mysterious, and beautiful place—Amman, Jordan.

When we landed, after our fourteen-hour direct flight from Chicago to Amman, we were understandably disoriented—not only because of the length of the flight but also because of the scene at the airport. There, before us, was absolute chaos posing as the visa line. It wasn't so much a line as it was a fight to get to the counter. Arabs, we would learn, don't queue. Once we figured this out, we fought our way to the counter and got our visas to enter the country of Jordan. It was that easy back then. Just walk up to the counter with your passport, and, as Americans, get a stamp.

Rick picked us up at the airport and drove us the long distance from the airport to a house church at some strangers' apartment. Something about going to a house church in the Middle East felt mysterious and dangerous to us. That was one of many misconceptions about the Middle East that was dismantled during this journey. Not only were there many house churches, but there were actual church buildings with as many denominations as there were in Pekin—Catholic, Orthodox, Nazarene, Evangelical Free, and so on. The Church began in the Middle East, we were reminded, and has been there since the beginning of the common era. We were free to worship as Christians despite being a small minority. We had a lot to learn.

On the way, through the vast metropolis of Amman, we noticed a teenage Muslim girl wearing hijab (a Muslim headscarf) and skin-tight jeans. This was another of the many occasions in which we realized that our stereotypes of the Middle East were completely incorrect. With Omar as my framework, whose religion required him to read his holy book in a foreign language, the tight-jeaned hijabi did not compute.

On our first night, we were awakened by the sound of the call to prayer, resounding in a terribly treble-heavy tone from a minaret not too far from the apartment where we were staying. "*Allahu Akbar*!" (God is greater!) It was truly a rude awakening. My wife began to sob. "What have we gotten ourselves into?"

I, being the ever-loving, gracious husband that I always have been, said, "I don't know, but we're kind of stuck here for four months, so…"

The truth was that neither of us knew what we had gotten ourselves into. We were on an adventure that we were utterly unprepared for.

The next morning, Rick drove us what felt like another eternity, from the posh neighborhood of Sweifiyya to the ghetto of Jebel Ashrafiyya. He had arranged a furnished apartment for us in the building of Umm Sa'ad (mother of Sa'ad), a Christian woman who lived there. He dropped us off, introduced us to Umm Sa'ad, who spoke very little English, and said, "This is your neighborhood. Go explore! We will see you on Friday." Then he drove away, leaving us a million miles away from anyone or anything that we knew. All we had was a piece of paper with some transliterated Arabic words to help us find his apartment "near the Egyptian Embassy"; the ability to ask, "Do you speak English?" in Arabic; and our sense of adventure. We were completely alone.

This was the beginning of my education.

The English Center

Part of our work (as volunteers) during the first few months of our time in Jordan was at an English center run by a Christian organization, as I mentioned earlier. At the center, we taught

English-as-a-second-language (ESL) classes for a minimal fee. It was a luxury to learn English from first-language speakers, and usually that opportunity was not afforded to anyone but the wealthiest of individuals. What the center provided was a cheap and quality English education to average people. The students seemingly ignored the fact that the center was run by Christians and attended classes anyway. This translated to the student population reflecting the population of Jordan; the students were probably 97 percent Muslim. It was just like my high school in Pekin, except this time, *I* was the minority.

One evening, the center was hosting a "Conversation Night" for the students. As a completely ignorant American Christian, I was excited to finally sit around a table with students and talk about religion and politics. I knew practically nothing about either of these topics, and as a learner, I was eager to engage in real conversations and hear what the students thought about God or about Israel or whatever else might come up. I had a difficult time during our first few months in Jordan finding relational outlets. Being an extrovert in a foreign country in which most people don't speak your language can be a bit depressing. I was hoping that this night would lead to some friendships for me, outside of class.

My hopes were dashed when this turned into a "guided discussion" on "spiritual peace." We were all herded into groups with discussion leaders and forced to listen to an allegory of a man on a quest for spiritual peace. He couldn't find this peace no matter how

25

hard he tried. Even worse, no answers were given for how one might find it. The purpose of this guided discussion was solely to discover which students were "open to the gospel." I was frustrated, because I wanted to have actual conversations about real issues and even more because I simply hated the idea. I was only a volunteer at this center, but as a Christian, I was complicit with this idea even though I had no idea it was happening and didn't approve of the method. Having been raised in a highly evangelism-focused Baptist church, I saw this as an attempt to evangelize and convert the students who attended the English center. It was as if the English classes were a bait and switch to force Muslim students to confront the mysteries of the gospel.

The Muslims in the group were on guard, as they were also well aware of what was happening. In the words of the infamous T. Jarrett Harris, "Sometimes God blesses bad ideas. I just don't want to be a part of this one." These words were running through my head as discomfort and agitation filled the room.

There was an awkward young man in our breakout group whom I had not yet met. He was skinny and pale and had braces and a raspy, high-pitched voice. At some point in the discussion, an argument started between him and some of the other students in the group about his religious identity. Apparently, his way of speaking wasn't orthodox or Muslim enough for the other students. He was asked, "Are you even a Muslim?" To this, he responded, "What does it matter what I say that I am? I am searching for truth." My interest

26

was piqued. I needed to know what he meant, as a Muslim, by being on a search for truth. After all, how does a Muslim in a Muslim country search and find truth as a Muslim? What does that look like? And what does he mean by being on a search for truth?

After the discussion ended, I went up to introduce myself to the young man, whose name was Jamal. "I would be interested in hearing about your search for truth," I said. It was true. I had no desire to talk about my own search for truth or to twist the conversation into one about how Jesus is the truth or anything of the sort. I genuinely wanted to know what that search looked like for him and how he was going about it.

"I don't want to talk about that. I want to know how I can find *spiritual peace*," Jamal replied. Turns out, the discussion *had* stirred something in Jamal, and he wanted answers.

The problem was he was talking with me, a guy who wasn't interested in giving answers at all. So, I replied, "I don't know how you're going to find spiritual peace." As the words came out of my mouth, I thought about how lame that response was. He was inviting me into the very conversation that I had hoped for at the beginning of the night, and I was backing down. My aversion to evangelism, which was nurtured in the church in which I was raised, had kept me from wanting to share my perspective with Jamal. I didn't want to talk about my experience of faith because, from my perspective, it was irrelevant. After all, he was Muslim.

"I mean…I could tell you how I find spiritual peace," I said as awkwardly as humanly possible. I was unconvincing. I wouldn't ever have had a conversation about *spiritual peace.* That phrase bore no meaning for me, then as now. I didn't want to imply that I was uninterested in him or in conversation, so I went for it. Jamal apparently decided that this conversation was worth his time, and we found an empty table at the center and entered into a conversation— one that I was completely unprepared for.

I dove into the deep end with Jamal, telling him about all that was fascinating about what I had recently been learning. I told him about the story of reconciliation and redemption that God has been writing throughout all of human history. I told him about how I saw Jesus showing up in Abraham's story and in Moses's story. I wasn't at all telling him about how I found spiritual peace, at least not in my estimation. I was simply letting him in on something that I thought was particularly exciting and interesting. This was my framework for understanding everything that I saw in the world, and I was telling him about my framework.

At the same time, I started thinking about the consequences of this conversation I was having with Jamal. Like I mentioned, Jordan is 97 percent Muslim, and as such, there were laws against proselytizing. Specifically, if I was caught having such a conversation with Jamal, despite my intention (which was definitely not to proselytize or convert him), I could be kicked out of the country. Given that, coupled with the fact that I had just met Jamal *and* the fact that I didn't want to have this conversation in the first place, I asked him if he wanted to go to my apartment. I didn't want to get kicked out of the country for this kid, at least not yet. I would feel safer for both of us if we could have this conversation behind closed doors rather than in the public setting at the center.

Oddly enough, given the circumstances, Jamal took me up on it, and we headed up the staircases built into Jebel Ashrafiyya from the downtown city center. When we got to my apartment, I pulled a Bible off of my bookshelf, opened it, and started flipping to different scriptures. I was completely clueless as to what I was doing or hoping for. I was simply compelled to share what I was learning with Jamal. I remember specifically flipping to Zephaniah, a book that I had not read and have not since read (at least as I recall). I don't know what I read to him from Zephaniah, but I'm sure it was fascinating. I wasn't trying to convince Jamal. I was telling him why *I* was convinced.

I think there is a world of difference between those two statements.

A person who is trying to convince another person that his or her way of seeing or believing is true tends to look at the other person as a person in need of a new road map. He or she is lost, and I need to convince him or her to look at a new map in order to move from lost-ness to found-ness. A person who is convinced of something and sharing that conviction with another is like a person sharing a new recipe with someone else. To create a metaphor, if we say that God is a cucumber and faith is what one does with that cucumber in order to make it taste good, then I was sharing with Jamal that my faith adds tomatoes and tzatziki sauce to the cucumber and all I was doing was inviting him to try it to see what it tasted like.

I finally came to a passage in Galatians that read, "There is no longer Jew or Greek, there is no longer slave or free, there is no longer male and female; for all of you are one in Christ Jesus. And if you belong to Christ, then you are Abraham's offspring, heirs according to the promise."[7] For me, it was a rather benign set of verses. I had heard them in various contexts throughout my lifetime. There was nothing particularly spectacular or groundbreaking about these verses for me.

However, Jamal's eyes began to tear up as he exclaimed, "This is good news! Everyone needs to hear this!"

I was floored. I looked around the room, wondering what had just happened, and said, "That's what it's called."

Jamal was Muslim. In hearing these words, he identified them as "good news," which was precisely what *gospel* means. And, perhaps more significantly for me, he said that this "good news" needed to be heard by everyone, which meant all Muslims. It was as

---

[7] Galatians 3:27–29 (New Revised Standard Version).

if Jamal had tasted the cucumber, tomato, and tzatziki combination and said, "This is delicious! Everyone needs to taste this!"

Again, I realized that I didn't have a framework for what I had just heard. Was it even possible that the good news was actually good news for everyone—not just for Christians, but for everyone? I had suspected it was, and I had taught others that it was, but I had never really *believed* or *seen* that it was. I am a Christian, born into a Christian context, who received a Christian message that was good for Christians to the general exclusion of everyone else after all. Whether I believed it or not, this was my foundation.

And what is the good news that Jamal heard? I've asked myself this question many times over the years. I know that many people hear this story and hear me say that Jamal heard about Jesus for the first time and believed it as good news and that was the most important point. That may be part of it. But, as a Muslim, Jamal was familiar with Jesus, with Abraham, and with Moses. He wasn't hearing about Jesus for the first time that night. He knew Jesus.

I think the good news Jamal heard and believed that night was that there is reconciliation with God in the end that is good for everyone. All people become one again. Our sad divisions will cease. If that's not the basis of the good news that Jamal heard, I'm sure it is a portion. Regardless, that night, Jamal blew apart my foundation and laid a new one. That new foundation was based on a realization that somehow, through a conversation as friends, we could truly experience something mutually life changing and life giving. Jamal's openness to learning showed me that Muslims aren't closed off to relationships with Christians. He showed me that we aren't as different as we perceive ourselves to be and in other ways, we are worlds apart. He showed me that these differences don't have to be barriers to relationships.

We had many more conversations after that night about faith; about following Jesus as a Muslim; about conversion from one religious system to another religious system and whether or not that was the point; about family, fear, and Islam; and about how Muslims and Christians might engage in friendship despite our differences.

One night, I asked Jamal to explain to me why in the Qur'an it states, "And you will surely find that the nearest in amity toward the believers are those who say: 'We are Christians,'" and later it states, "O believers, do not take unbelievers for allies apart from the believers."[8] I saw an apparent contradiction in these two verses: that Christians are closest in heart to Muslims, and on the contrary, Muslims should not ally themselves with Christians. Jamal explained that these two chapters were revealed at different times, one during a time of peace and one during a time of war. This is a common response to such a question—context matters in Islam as much as it does in Christianity. There isn't an easy way to verify whether Jamal was right in his understanding of the contexts of the two Qur'anic

---

[8] Qur'an 5:82 and 4:144, Tarif Khalidi, trans.

verses, but that's beside the point. In its simplicity, it made sense to me.

I took the conversation to the next level and asked, "So, if America attacks Jordan (for no apparent reason), are you my friend?" I was asking him which was more important to him, our friendship or what his faith community might require. It was probably an unfair question.

"I don't know," he replied—a simple, honest response. I believe that Jamal was and is my friend. His response told me that faith and friendship across lines of difference are complicated, as we are all well aware.

There is no doubt that Jamal found something invigorating and faith-inducing through our conversations. There is no doubt that I found much the same thing as a result of our time together. There is no doubt that we became friends, true friends, despite the narrative that says because he is a Muslim and I am a Christian we are enemies. There is no doubt that I became a better version of myself and that he became a better version of himself as a result.

I asked him a few years later what it was about our first conversations that he found so compelling. He replied, "You shared with me that Jesus said build your house on rock (be sure about what you believe)."

We never talked about that.

Jamal is reading the Bible and figuring out what it means to be a true Muslim (one who is submitted to God) through the words of Jesus on his own. The Bible has become a source of truth for Jamal that helps him become a better version of himself. As we have engaged in a dialogical friendship, he has added the commitment to understanding the Bible as scripture as a part of his experience of faith as a Muslim. Likewise, I have taken on the commitment of searching for and celebrating truth in the Qur'an as a part of my experience of faith as a Christian.

Jamal never became a Christian. But that's not the point. Jamal and I remain friends, engaged in a dialogical friendship in which we are still challenging one another to become better versions of ourselves as we search for truth together.

It is a beautiful thing.

Interlude

Ahmed

Hope broke out one night in Irvine, California. On this particular night, that hope came to me in the form of a man named Ahmed. He was a fellow graduate student, and he was studying for law school while I was reading for my master's in theology at the café that I think he owns. After I asked him what he was reading, he asked me about my reading, at which point I told him I was studying for my MA in theology.

Ahmed said, "Theology. That has something to do with God, right?"

I told him that it technically *is* the study of God. Then he asked me if I believed in God, and again I answered in the affirmative. He said it was refreshing to meet someone who still believed in God.

Then he asked me what I made of all of the religions. "Are they all man-made, or are they from God?"

I told Ahmed that I believed all religions were seeking to speak of the mysteries of God in particular ways. I said that they were different because they were seeking to answer different questions and the problem between religions was that we had difficulty in embracing the similarities because of these different framing questions.

Seemingly intrigued, Ahmed then asked me if I believed in the miracles of the prophets. He asked me if I believed that Moses parted the Red Sea. I told Ahmed that the question wasn't a matter of whether the Red Sea was actually parted, but whether it told us something true about God. That's the power of such a story. Stories like this don't necessarily have to be *proven* or *believed* to be literally or factually true because they still tell us something true about God. The reality is that if the Red Sea *did* part, Moses didn't do it, but God did. In this instance, the story tells us that God is about redemption and about setting the relationship between himself and this particular people back to rights. In this way, I can say that I believe that Moses parted the Red Sea because I believe that the story behind that story is true to my experience and my desire for the way I hope life really may be—that God is indeed a God who redeems us.

I went on to tell Ahmed why I believed the Bible was the truest of the stories, explaining about the two trees in the creation story. Because Adam and Eve broke the relationship that they had with God, God showed mercy toward them by protecting them from eternal life in this broken state by kicking them out of the mythical garden and keeping them from eating of the tree of life. I told Ahmed that the interesting thing about the story of the Bible was that the tree of life showed up in the ending too. And, in the end, after God had finally put everything back to rights, the tree of life was for the healing of the nations, so we would live forever in right relationship with the Creator in the end. I said that I believed that was the best story to live by.

Ahmed then said that he thought that if we had miracles today, we would see more people believing in God. I disagreed. I told him the parable/myth/story of Lazarus and the rich man that Jesus told. Ultimately, Abraham told the rich man that if his brothers didn't understand and believe Moses, sending Lazarus back from the dead to warn them of impending judgment would be of no use. They wouldn't believe in that sign either. Then I showed him how this was exemplified in Jesus's own life. Jesus fed five thousand people with a few loaves and some fish, and the next event described in the book of John is the people asking Jesus to give them a sign. Then Jesus cryptically called himself the true bread and made himself sound like a vampire-diet promoter, after which all of the people deserted him. Jesus asked his disciples if they too would desert him, and Peter said, "Where would we go, for you have the words that bring life?"[9] I told Ahmed that the point of this story was that true faith didn't demand a sign but believed the words because they brought life to the hearer.

Ahmed told me that he had never heard answers like the ones I had given him and that he had always wondered about these things. He said that I gave him something to think about and that I should write a book. I told him that there were plenty of books.

---

[9] John 6:68, *paraphrased*.

He then told me about how Christians had hurt him personally in the past and how he had become disillusioned with religion altogether, being a Muslim but not a practicing one. All of this happened because I had asked him what he was studying and he reciprocated. I often miss these chances at truly important, meaningful, life-giving, mutual conversations because I don't take the chance at even having a conversation in the first place. Even though they are "neighbors," I am more prone to ignore the people around me than I am to actually get to know their stories, let alone have a significant and instantly deep conversation like the one I had with Ahmed.

I'm glad that night, by the grace of God, I paid attention.

2
Neighbors

He who believes in Allah and the Last Day should either utter good words
or better keep silence; and he who believes in Allah and the Last Day
should treat his neighbor with kindness and he who believes in Allah and
the Last Day should show hospitality to his guest. - *Sahih Bukhari*, vol. **8**,
bk. 73, nos. 47 and 158.

You shall not hate in your heart anyone of your kin, you shall reprove your
neighbor, or you will incur guilt yourself. You shall not take vengeance or
bear a grudge against any of your people, but you shall love your neighbor
as yourself: I am the LORD. - Leviticus 19:17–18 (NRSV).

In everything do to others as you would have them do to you; for this is the
law and the prophets. - Matthew 7:12 (NRSV).

Divided Humanity

We live in an incredibly divided world. We divide on almost every front—politics, sports teams, national and state boundaries, racial and ethnic lines, sexual orientation, craft or domestic beer, diet plans, parenting strategies, and not least of all, religious lines (and even within religions, we have denominations, sects, and schools). This phenomenon of division takes place in urban centers where there are "districts" in which similar people have chosen to live near one another. Chicago famously has neighborhoods like Chinatown and Boys Town, but there are also enclaves in the city of Arabs, Greeks, blacks, and whites. In other cities, one could relatively easily guess the racial background of an anonymous person based solely upon his or her zip code. It is perfectly natural, or so it seems, for humans to choose to live around, worship with, and rally alongside people with whom we share interests, identities, and cultural affinities.

The problem with these divisions that seem so natural, however, is that they cause us to separate ourselves from people who don't think/believe/act the way we do. When we start *othering* people who don't look or think like us, we steal something from them—their basic humanity. What I mean by *basic humanity* is what Jews, Christians, and many Muslims refer to as the divine image, the image of God, or the breath of God that all humans share—whether straight or gay; male or female; white or black; Indian or indigenous American; Christian, Jew, or Muslim. When *we* are "normal," then anyone who is not like us is *not* "normal." The *other* then takes on the form of something less than human. We lump individuals into groups, and we mindlessly go through our lives ignoring (at best) and demonizing (at worst) those groups with which we don't identify. And "when our clans, castes, and civilizations teach generation after generation of children to hold oppositional identities, rendering them hostile towards other people who have been raised in their respective identity tents, then our clans and castes and civilizations must be repented of, including our Christian clans and castes and civilizations."[10] This reality led Lee Camp to ask, "How can I possibly love one to whom I refuse to even listen? How can I possibly love one whose viewpoint or experience I refuse to grant even a hearing?"[11] Our isolation has created such an environment.

Truthfully, we have cultivated our ability to hate our neighbors as a culture and have lost almost all semblance of creativity when it comes to loving them. Almost every non-Muslim knows that one of the easiest ways to hate a Muslim neighbor (and instigate a fight) is to draw a cartoon of the Prophet Muhammad. One may recall how Pamela Geller of the American Freedom Defense Initiative played a role in creating such a contest in Garland, Texas, under the guise of free speech. This was followed by a protest by a group of anti-Muslim bikers at a mosque in Phoenix, Arizona, where the bikers

---

[10] Brian D. McLaren, *Why Did Jesus, Moses, the Buddha, and Mohammed Cross the Road? Christian Identity in a Multi-Faith World* (New York: Jericho Books, 2012), 259.

[11] Lee Camp, *Who Is My Enemy? Questions American Christians Must Face about Islam—and Themselves* (Grand Rapids: Brazos Press, 2011), 8.

held an impromptu cartoon-drawing contest and then brought the cartoons to taunt the Muslims entering the mosque for prayer. There is no possibility that these actions were benign. One cannot accidentally draw such a cartoon. Admittedly, it is an intensely creative display of hatred.

There is a theological reason why the act of making an image of the Prophet Muhammad is offensive and an act of hatred to many Muslims. First, Muslims believe that God is the Creator of everything, and some take that to mean that even creating an image of anything is blasphemous. If you recall the story of the Israelites and the golden calf in Exodus, you get a sense of this aversion to creating images. Many Muslims believe this can lead to idolatry. This is why the artwork that Muslim communities are known for is calligraphy—making beautiful images out of the words of the Qur'an. Second, Muslims deeply revere the Prophet Muhammad, seeking to emulate him in word and deed. "If something is felt by Muslims to be a denigration of...Muhammad, then by implication such may be seen as an attack on the whole way of life of each and every Muslim."[12] When non-Muslims make cartoon images of the Prophet Muhammad, typically cast in a negative light, it is considered to be an attack on all Muslims.

On the contrary, if you ask average Christians how they can show love to their Muslim neighbors, you might get a blank stare.

---

[12] Andrew Rippin, *Muslims: Their Religious Beliefs and Practices*, 4th ed. (London: Routledge, 2012), 52.

Instead of finding creative ways to actively and openly demonstrate love for our neighbors, we have spent our time and creativity on actively and openly hating them. This is what happens when we let fear of the other fester inside of us.

The problem with these creative displays of neighbor hatred is that our religions' greatest prophets—Moses, Jesus, and Muhammad—exhorted us to a different way of being in the world among our neighbors. Collectively, however, it seems these words have fallen on deaf ears. In an attempt to resurrect an open discussion on what it means to be a faithful person in a multifaith world, the first place to turn is the greatest command—to love our neighbors as we love ourselves.

The Middle

The love of one's neighbor was the impetus for *A Common Word* and the subsequent *Yale Response*, two academic documents written and signed by Muslim and Christian scholars with the purpose of opening up a robust dialogue between the two religious groups. Traditionally, Judaism has seen the command to love one's neighbor as the pinnacle of the pinnacle of the pinnacle of the Torah.[13] Jesus said that there are two commands, the love of God and the love of neighbor, on which the entire Torah hang.[14] To understand what he was saying in a Jewish context, we need to go back to Leviticus

---

[13] More will be said about the pinnacle of the pinnacle of the pinnacle in what follows.

[14] Matthew 22:40 (NRSV).

and get a sense of the importance the command to love our neighbors as ourselves had when it was originally given to the ancient Israelites.

In the Jewish and Christian canon (or arrangement) of Scripture, Leviticus is the third book. There are five books that make up the Torah (or Pentateuch): Genesis, Exodus, Leviticus, Numbers, and Deuteronomy. Despite containing various genres of literature, these books are viewed primarily as law books. Leviticus, as the third of the five books, is considered the pinnacle of the Torah, both literally and figuratively.[15] Within Leviticus, the nineteenth chapter, though not technically the middle chapter, is considered to be the pinnacle of the book.[16] In chapter 19 of Leviticus, there are thirty-seven verses. The middle verse, 18, says this: "You shall not take vengeance or bear a grudge against any of your people, but you shall love your neighbor as yourself: I am the LORD." So, when Jesus implies that the entire Torah hangs on this commandment, he sees "love your neighbor" as the pinnacle of the pinnacle of the pinnacle of the Torah. Every other command and story in the entire Torah hangs from this single commandment.

This is a significant literary clue, especially in ancient literature. For writers and readers in the ancient Near East, the middle of a section of literature was often the main point. All of the

---

[15] Richard S. Briggs and Joel N. Lohr, eds. *A Theological Introduction to the Pentateuch: Interpreting the Torah as Christian Scripture* (Grand Rapids: Baker Academic, 2012), 87.

[16] See Mary Douglas's article in the journal *Interpretation* 53, no. 4 (1999).

other content either rose or fell from the middle. This is called a *chiasm*. In modern Western literature, the climax is often found near the end of a piece of literature or Hollywood movie. Imagine if the spinning top at the end of *Inception* was actually the middle scene. Not only would we leave the theater with little to talk about, because we would actually find out if it did topple over, it would seem that we would then have learned too much. Since we are used to looking to the end of a script or a text for the climax, we often miss the significance of chiasms in ancient literature. What is remarkable about this verse in Leviticus is that it is to be seen and understood as the ultimate middle of an ultimate chiasm. All of the Torah literally rises to and falls from this one command. This one verse is the ultimate climax in Scripture!

If that were all that could be said, it might be enough to convince us that this command matters, at least to Jews and to Christians. Rabbi Hillel, who was alive the century prior to Jesus, said that Leviticus 19:18 means, "[That] which is hateful to you, do not do to your fellow," and claimed that he saw it as the central tenant of Scripture and even Judaism.[17] And when Jesus said, "In everything do to others as you would have them do to you; for this is the law and the prophets," he was likely commenting on this verse as well as R. Hillel's interpretation of it.[18] Notice Jesus claims that this *is* the law and the prophets—a fairly all-encompassing statement.

---

[17] Jacob D. Milgrom, *Leviticus: A Book of Ritual and Ethics* (Minneapolis: Fortress Press, 2004), 233.
[18] Matthew 7:12 (NRSV).

It is no surprise that the Prophet Muhammad picked up on the importance of this command. He was living in community with Jews in Yathrib (Medina) during the beginning of his prophetic ministry in the Arabian Peninsula. He was also married to a Christian woman for more than twenty-five years.[19] So, when he said, "None of you has faith until you love for your neighbor what you love for yourself," he was interpreting the book of Moses (Tawrat or Torah) in a simple phrase.[20] This is evidence that at least a millennium after the book of Leviticus was put into its final form, Jews and Christians in the middle of a desert still were remembering and reminding others of the significance of this command to the life of faith. In his commentary on this hadith (traditional saying) of the Prophet Muhammad, HRH Prince Ghazi bin Muhammad wrote, "Without giving the neighbor what we ourselves love, we do not love God or the neighbor."[21] In other words, the law and the prophets, as well as the religions of Islam, Judaism, and Christianity, are all bound up in the command to love our neighbors as we love ourselves.

That is not to say that these commands hold the same importance for Muslims, Jews, and Christians today. I was recently talking with an Imam, and he said, "There are many Christians that are bent on hatred and violence." I didn't argue with him. There *are* many Christians who are living in complete opposition to the

---

[19] For an excellent historical summary of the genesis of Islam, see *No God but God* by Reza Aslan.
[20] *Sahih al-Bukhari, Kitab al-Iman*, no. 13.
[21] Volf, *A Common Word*, 44.

command to love their neighbors as they love themselves. Indeed, Christians are the most peace-loving people, quick to condemn violence when seen in another group of people, but are often more than willing to support war and violence when it comes to their own safety—a hypocrisy that others have noticed. It is a fair point. Christians over the centuries *have* largely ignored the command to love their neighbors as themselves.

The irony of the Imam's accusation, however, is that the same can be said about Islam and Muslims. Muhammad's words about giving love to our neighbors could not be further out of mind for ISIS, for instance. And what role do the Prophet's words play in suicide bombings in places like Yemen or Saudi Arabia, which are inflicted upon fellow Muslims? One day, I had a nine-year-old Muslim girl tell me that she once wanted to be a doctor, but now she wants to join the army and kill Israelis. At nine years old! What was the effect of Muhammad's words on her way of being in the world? That is not to say I would have responded any differently at her age. We can hardly hold a nine-year-old accountable for the way she may or may not have been taught by those around her to think about the world.

Consider also the Zionist Jewish settlers who are routinely bulldozing and stealing land from Palestinians in the West Bank. These Jews are going to their literal neighbors and taking everything they own away, along with their inherent dignity. The very wall built between Israel and the West Bank is evidence that these words of

47

Moses have not held sway over many Jewish minds. It is impossible to justify this action with the Torah, but that isn't even in view. The politics of our nations and tribes so often cloud the teachings of our faiths.

But these generalizations fall short as well. When I lived in Amman, Jordan, we had to find jobs after figuring out that we had not brought enough money to survive our initial four-month plan as volunteers. In a strange twist of fate, I taught for a year at an Islamic school called The School of Life, which was founded and administered by a princess. I taught English-language subjects like science, math, history, and health science. One day, in my fifth-grade health science class, we were talking about relationships—since health science is concerned with a healthy life, not just healthy bodies. I decided to write Jesus's words from Matthew 7:12—"In everything do to others as you would have them do to you"—on the whiteboard. I told my students that I would give 5 Jordanian dinars (JD) (roughly $7.50) to anyone who could tell me who said those words.

Admittedly, this was a ridiculous challenge. What was I trying to prove? Jesus or Moses is better than Muhammad?

My students yelled out that Muhammad had said this. I, being unaware of the hadith quoted above and attributed to the Prophet Muhammad, told them that someone had said this much earlier than Muhammad had.

This statement was met with fifteen blank stares on my students' faces.

I didn't follow through with telling them that Jesus had said, "In everything do to others as you would have them do to you," mostly because I was afraid of the ramifications. It isn't wise for a Christian teacher in an Islamic school in a Muslim country to trump the Prophet Muhammad with Jesus, regardless of the fact that Jesus is also a prophet in Islam. However, these fifth-graders *knew* that the Prophet Muhammad had said something like this. It was on their radar. It *was* important. These words, which still bear significance to Jews (as the heart of the Torah) and to Christians (as the meaning of the entire Old Testament) were also significant to these nine-year-old Muslim kids in health science class.

Regardless of how we view what is happening in the world, we at least have to say that on our best days, Muslims, Jews, and Christians want to be living in ways that are loving toward their neighbors. We *want* to be the hope in the world. We believe that this is at least *a* way toward peace in our world. What it will take for this hope for peace to be realized is a renewed commitment from all of us to creatively love our neighbors with the belief that since we have been commanded to live in this way with others, we might as well give it a shot and see what happens.

What Is Love?

Love is altogether and for ever on the alert, and it casts about to do some good even to one who is unwilling to receive it.

—Dionysius of Alexandria[22]

One difficulty with the command to love our neighbors is that *love* and *neighbor* are nebulous words at best. They don't bear just one meaning in English but many *meanings*. Take the word *love* for example. One can *love* Taylor Swift, pizza, dogs, and one's spouse, but we know that these loves are different. The love one has for salted caramel gelato is not the same as the love one has for one's children—or at least we hope not. But that's beside the point.

We don't choose to love our families or the foods that taste good to us. We just inherently love them. In this way, love is a state of being or a feeling, not an action. Sure, we act out our love for our children by hugging them or giving them good gifts, and we act out our love for pizza by eating it as often as possible, but familial love or affinity for a food item is not what the injunctions on Muslims, Jews, and Christians to love our neighbors mean.

"The true understanding of love of neighbor…is a type of love of neighbor that emerges from a great tree, the tree of the love of God. Love of God will lead us to love the creation of God. If you love the Creator, you will love what He created…I love my neighbor

---

[22] Camp, *Who Is My Enemy?*, 23.

because God chose my neighbor for me."[23] We don't choose our neighbors (no matter how much we may try). A Christian friend of mine told me that though she lives on a farm in the country, a Muslim family just moved into a house down the road (it should be noted that she was excited by that fact, not terrified). We are not in control of whom we find ourselves living near, working with, or going to school with. What the love of neighbor command requires of us is to love our neighbors precisely *because* they exist and because we love the Creator who created them.

But this *love* is *not* an idea. "The word *love* implies both attitude and act; one must not only feel love but also act in ways that translate love into concrete deeds. Just as one expresses love for God through active obedience to God's commandments, so one must demonstrate love for others by reaching out to them with tangible deeds of compassion and concern."[24] Take my neighbors, John and Joanna, for example. There are many, many things about John that annoy me—mostly how he seems to only have time to work on his broken-down motorcycle during nap or bedtime at my house. He will rev the engine, let it stall, and rev it some more, the sound of which literally shakes the walls of my house. In these moments, he is the worst kind of next-door neighbor. I don't *feel* love for John, at least most of the time, and definitely never while he is disturbing the

---

[23] Volf, *A Common Word*, 84.

[24] Samuel E. Balentine, *Leviticus: Interpretation* (Louisville: John Knox Press, 2002), 165.

peace in my house. We haven't shared any meals together. We don't hang out. We aren't what could be considered *friends*. But when he or his wife is in need of eggs or Advil or when we need cheese or a lawnmower, we don't hesitate to ask or to give. When the weather is bad, our basement is open to them. When we need a babysitter, their daughter is open to us. They care for our kids, and we care for theirs. We didn't choose each other, but we are neighbors, both literally and figuratively. In the most generic sense, we show love for one another through concrete actions for the good of each other. Though we haven't engaged in the act of really becoming friends, which is perhaps the ultimate goal of loving our neighbors, we are still open to one another, despite our annoying habits.

The word *love* found in Leviticus, in Hebrew *aheb*, is also not a complex word. It means simply "to love." It is translated in many ways, referring to lovers, friends, and others with whom we have close relationships. With its diverse use in the Hebrew language (like the word for love, *hib*, in Arabic), it is not much more helpful than our English word *love* in defining its meaning in various contexts. We know that the ancient Israelites didn't have the same type of love for their lover as they did their brothers. The word used for this command in Greek, however, is *agape*. *Agape* is a particular kind of love; it is more than brotherly (*phileo*), more than romantic (*eros*)— it is a love that transcends all boundaries. It is unconditional. This love is usually attributed to God himself. It is a love that gives, expecting nothing in return, and that loves even when it is not reciprocated. This is the way love toward our neighbors looks; it is easier said than done.

Indeed, we may not *feel* love toward our neighbors at all. We are more likely to ignore their existence than we are to feel love toward them. But at the heart of the word *love*, as it relates to loving our neighbors, is that it is more than a feeling; it is a way of being in the world that purposely and specifically acts on behalf of the other out of compassion and concern for his or her well-being. If for no other reason, we love our neighbors for they are created in the image of God, just like we are. Rabbi Ben Azzai, in the first century CE, understood the meaning of love in the Torah in this way: "First, make such a (and every) person aware that he is of ultimate worth because he bears the likeness of God, that regardless of his condition he has the divinely endowed potential to achieve joy and fulfillment in life, and only then, after having learned to love himself, will he be capable of loving others."[25] If we are able to look at our neighbors first as image-bearers of the divine and even more to assure them that this is the case, then we will mutually be able to love one another as we love ourselves. It will become clear in the following chapters that this basic understanding of humans in relation to God might be the key to how we change the way we interact with *all* people.

My friend Zach shared with me a story that was equal parts inspiring and challenging regarding a relationship he had with an

---

[25] Milgrom, *Leviticus*, 235.

incredibly difficult coworker at the restaurant he used to work in as a waiter. Restaurant work is notoriously cutthroat and competitive. Everyone is trying to get the best tables in order to receive the best tips. This coworker would regularly try to bully or manipulate the other waitstaff into letting her have what she considered to be the best tables. If you have ever been a waiter, you know that this is not an especially unique scenario. In a high-end restaurant, this can be the difference between a one-hundred-dollar shift and a two-hundred-dollar shift. But on slow nights, she would say that she felt sick and then try to manipulate her coworkers into taking over her closing shifts, leaving the others to suffer the demise of a nonlucrative shift. In this situation, it is easy and normal to dread working with such a person.

However, Zach was regularly being challenged to see every person as being created in the image of God and therefore worthy of our love and respect. Instead of taking the path of tough love and telling her how miserable she was making everyone around her, he sought to understand her situation. She was a longtime single parent who relied on her job as a waitress to provide for her teenage daughter. This didn't minimize the reality that Zach's income was also reliant on this job, but it allowed him to see her unique situation as at least part of her reason for being so competitive, harsh, and manipulative. When Zach began to see her first as created in the image of God rather than the worst coworker on the planet, he was able to *love her* despite her shortcomings and abrasiveness. This also made for a pleasanter working environment, because Zach began to see his coworker as a fellow image-bearer of the divine rather than a manipulative bully. He was able to love his neighbor/coworker as he loved himself, because she too was worthy of all love, dignity, and respect. We could learn a lot from his example.

And Who Is My Neighbor?

To live fully as a Muslim or Christian does not require anything less of us than loving the neighbor, whether he or she be Muslim or Christian, and it requires us not to ask, "Is he or she one of us?" but to recognize that "He or she is one of His."

—Seyyed Hossein Nasr[26]

In the Gospel of Luke, we find Jesus in a conversation with a lawyer. A lawyer in Jesus's day was particularly familiar with the Torah, as practicing law meant knowing *the Law* in the first century. The lawyer, when asked by Jesus what he thought was the greatest command, referenced the verse we are considering from Leviticus. Jesus told the lawyer that if he did these things, if he truly loved his neighbor and God, he would have life. The lawyer then issued a challenge to Jesus, asking, "And who is my neighbor?"[27] This is a question that had been and remains to be a source of debate among all of us. Throughout the history of Israel and Judaism, that question has also been asked and answered in various ways. Some understand

---

[26] Volf, *A Common Word*, 117.
[27] Luke 10:29 (NRSV).

that *neighbor* means one's fellow Jew (or a member of one's own tribe). Others have a more all-inclusive understanding that *neighbor* refers to all of humanity. This debate is not unique to Judaism. Muslims and Christians have also picked apart and argued this question throughout our histories. As we will see in chapter 3, Jesus answered this question as a rabbi in a particular way with a story that challenges the best of us today.

How are *we* supposed to understand the meaning of the word *neighbor*? In America, we often think of our neighbors as those five to eight families whose houses surround our house. These sixteen to forty people are our neighbors, to the exclusion of almost everyone else. With this understanding, John, Charles, the guy who swore at my friend Zach when we first moved in, the old couple whose names I have forgotten, and Glen, along with their families, are my neighbors.[28] While this is a helpful starting point to understanding who exactly is our neighbor, it's just that—a starting point. It is too focused on a literal understanding of an American suburban concept of neighbor.

In ancient Israel, it is likely that the original connotation for the word *neighbor* was one's fellow Israelite. A distant neighbor might be a member of another tribe of Israel, but in a literal understanding, one's neighbor was a member of one's own tribe and even one's own immediate household (which could contain up to forty people).[29] The

---

[28] Jay Pathak and Dave Runyon wrote *The Art of Neighboring* based on this concept.

word *rea* in Hebrew means fellow, friend, and companion, which serves to solidify this point; one's neighbor is a member of one's own tribe. In a tribal and patrilocal society, there is no doubt that the command to love one's neighbor was understood to be a command to live amicably, generously, and at peace with the members of the tribe.

If we were to impute this understanding of neighbor on our own tribes, we would understand our neighbors to be our families, our friends, and people with whom we worship. Although this is a slightly more nuanced understanding of *neighbor* than the American suburban concept of next-door neighbors, it is still rather limiting. In this understanding, a Muslim's neighbor is his or her fellow Muslim, a Jew's neighbor is his or her fellow Jew, and a Christian's neighbor is his or her fellow Christian. More specifically, a Sunni Muslim's neighbor is his or her fellow Sunni Muslim, a Shi'a Muslim's neighbor is his or her fellow Shi'a Muslim, an Orthodox Jew's neighbor is his or her fellow Orthodox Jew, a Reformed Jew's neighbor is his or her fellow Reformed Jew, a Protestant Christian's neighbor is his or her fellow Protestant Christian, a Catholic Christian's neighbor is his or her fellow Catholic Christian, and so on. Indeed, these distinctions aren't even enough (if we are being completely honest). If it were up to us, our *neighbor* would be anyone who looks, thinks, believes, and acts the same way that we do. In fact, one early rabbinic interpretation of this command stated,

---

[29] For more on patrilocal culture, see *The Epic of Eden* by Sandra Richter, 34–37.

"If [your neighbor] acts as your people do, you shall love him, but if not you shall not love him."[30] That is a very small group of people indeed.

Maimonides, who was the author of the Mishnah Torah, a twelfth-century CE interpretation of the Torah, restricted his interpretation of *neighbor* in Leviticus to the "brother in the Torah and the commandments," limiting the meaning of neighbor to observant Jews.[31] Though this may have been one traditional understanding of the meaning of *neighbor* in the Torah, it is not the only understanding. The final editors of the works of Rabbi Nathan, writing a full millennia before Maimonides, "have associated the commandment to love one's neighbor with the universal idea of humanity."[32] Humanity is a much broader group than one's own tribe, which is obvious. The reason given for this all-encompassing understanding of *neighbor* is as follows: since all human beings are bearers of God's image, the word *neighbor* should be understood to mean all humanity. "And you shall love your neighbor, for he is like you, equal to you and similar to you, for he too has been created in God's image and behold, he is a man like you."[33] What if we were to think the same way?

According to Muslim scholar Seyyed Hossein Nasr, we are no

---

[30] Reinhard Neudecker, "'And You Shall Love Your Neighbor as Yourself—I Am the Lord' (Lev. 19, 18) in Jewish Interpretation," *Biblica* 73, no. 4 (1992): 500.
[31] Ibid., 501.
[32] Ibid., 502.
[33] Ibid., 506.

longer able to think of our neighbors as being restricted to those of our own tribe. "Today, it cannot include for Muslims only Muslim neighbors, for Christians only Christian neighbors, or for Jews only Jewish neighbors. It must also include followers of other religious communities, even nonreligious communities, and especially the nonhuman world."[34] In our ever-shrinking multifaith world, with people from all religions and races in our communities, our neighbors have *become* all people—whether we like it or not. "[Since] God's love is unconditional and indiscriminate, human beings ought to love all their neighbors, the ones who belong to their 'group'…as well as those who do not, and those who are friendly to them as well as those who are not."[35]

This concept of loving neighbors who are friendly and those who are not is beautifully expressed in the following story, attributed to the life of the Prophet Muhammad.

> He had a neighbor who was in the habit of pelting him with objects and throwing things in his way whenever he went out for his five daily prayers. It so happened that one day the Prophet passed by the home of this neighbor, but he was not pelted with objects as usual. The man was not even there. Upon enquiry the Prophet learned that the man was sick, and he went into the man's home to wish him well. The neighbor was very surprised, as he had never thought he could be a recipient of the Prophet's good wishes. Then and there, he embraced Islam.[36]

---

[34] Volf, *A Common Word*, 116.
[35] Ibid., 71.

The point of this story is not primarily that the man converted to Islam. The point is that whether or not a person is good or evil, we are enjoined to love him or her as a neighbor—to act in tangible and concrete ways for his or her well-being because this person is human, just like us.

Though we might intuitively *know* that we are to love our good neighbors and our evil neighbors the same, the question begging to be asked is: Are we really supposed to love evil people? What about people, even neighbors, who commit atrocious and unthinkable crimes? Loving these people is counterintuitive to our normal way of being in the world. John S. Dickerson, a contributor to *USA Today*, related this story of forgiveness and love, as he reflected on its power to overcome evil and to instill hope that another way is possible even in the face of unspeakably evil neighbors.

> Last August, I listened to a recorded phone call with a pastor in Iraq. Islamic State terrorists had encircled his city, and he expected they would soon be headed to his church—to enforce their own murderous hatred upon him and his church members. Through tears, the Iraqi Christian prayed these words to his God: ISIS doesn't know what they are doing, so please forgive them.[37]

We expect evil to be met with resistance, not love. Like the story of

---

[36] Ibid., 120.

[37] "Charleston Victims Wield Power of Forgiveness: Column," *USA Today*, last modified June 22, 2015, accessed July 23, 2015, http://www.usatoday.com/story/opinion/2015/06/21/charleston-church-shooting-families-forgiveness-column/29069731.

Muhammad related above, this Iraqi pastor chose to believe that the only hope we have for peace and change is for us to live in a different way—to refuse to resist evil with evil means but to overcome evil with good. Love is disarming. When we see it, we know that we have encountered something truly powerful, especially in the face of great evil. When we actually *do* it, we choose to live according to a different narrative, one of hope and love rather than fear and hatred.

Knowing and Loving in Particular

It's one thing to say you love humanity in general, whatever their religion; it's quite another to learn to love this or that specific neighbor with his or her specific religion.

—Brian

McLaren[38]

Whether we understand our neighbors to be the people who live directly to our left or right, front or back, or we understand our neighbors to be all humanity is irrelevant. What matters is how we engage in relationships with people whom we know specifically, no matter their faith or their color. Though we can say that all humanity is encompassed in the idea of *neighbor*, that understanding can easily lead us into a general apathy toward people in particular. Perhaps the better question is: How do I love this particular person as he or she is, because of (not in spite of) our differences?

---

[38] McLaren, *Why Did Jesus...?*, 231.

My next-door neighbors may be my neighbors, but they also may not be, depending on the contact I have with them. For me, the guy across the street whose name I still have not learned in three years is not my neighbor, according to this definition. He is a stranger, or perhaps an enemy, but he is not currently my neighbor because I don't even know his name. My friends are my neighbors, as well as the people with whom I worship on Sunday mornings. The people I play soccer with on Sundays and the staff at the local coffee shop where I do most of my work are also my neighbors.

Neighbors don't necessarily have beliefs in common, but they do share common space or common activities. My neighbors don't all look or think like I do, but because of the regularity of our contact, I am given more opportunities to love them—by listening to their stories, acting on their behalf, and showing compassion and mercy toward them.

One of my neighbors, George, is an Anglican priest. We have never specifically spent time together as friends (I've never been to his house or his church, and he has never been to mine). However, we both work out of the same coffee shop, we have been at two birthday parties together, and we both play soccer in the same league. One Sunday afternoon, while playing soccer, George was kicked so hard in the ankle that he fell to the ground, cursing like a sailor (which is an endearing quality in a priest). On the sideline, I went over to George and offered to give him a ride home if he didn't feel like he would be able to drive. He didn't take me up on it, but that doesn't matter. Neighbor-love is willing to act concretely on behalf of the other.

One spring, I was in Irvine, California, for an intensive week of my master's program. The third night of the week, after ten hours of class, I pulled into a café that I had been studying at after hours. I parked incredibly poorly, so I got back into my car in order to straighten it out (no one likes a guy who takes up two spaces in a parking lot). Inexplicably, my car wouldn't start. It wouldn't even click, let alone turn over. There I was, thousands of miles away from home, stranded at night among a bunch of people I didn't know. I was neighborless. I *had* made a connection with the owner of the café earlier that week, so I decided to go inside and sit down for a while, let the car cool down, and hope to see him. The situation only got worse for me. As luck would have it, it was the owner's birthday and they were having a celebration in his honor, essentially eliminating the possibility that I could ask him for help. After all, it was *his* night.

After a couple of hours and still no luck, I had lost hope. I was in the process of figuring out how I would get my car towed somewhere, how I would get back to my hotel, *and* how I would get back to class the next morning, when, out of nowhere, Brett showed up. At this point, Brett and I were strangers (we will talk more about strangers in the following chapter). And for no apparent reason, he offered to help. He jumped my car and then followed me back to my hotel. When I parked at the hotel, again, the car was dead. Brett had done his part, but he wasn't finished. He was intent on making me into a neighbor. He gave me his phone number and told me that if my car didn't start in the morning to give him a call. Sure enough, the car didn't start in the morning so I reluctantly called him. About thirty minutes later, he showed up at the hotel with his jumper cables. He helped me get going once again and lent me his cables in case I had any more problems. But that's not the end of the story.

Two nights later, Brett gave me a call, inquiring about my car. I had taken it to a shop earlier in the day, and it was in the process of getting fixed. He asked if he could come by and pick up his cables, and when he arrived a third time at my hotel, he asked me if I was doing anything that night. He knew I was in town for school and that I had no people to hang out with. Brett invited me to hang out with him and his friends that evening. I had no reason to decline his offer of companionship and spent the rest of the evening surrounded by new friends I would have never met if it weren't for Brett's willingness to put compassion into action as a neighbor, loving me as himself.

During World War II, when Yugoslavia was invaded by the German forces, one Jewish family (among many), the Kavilios, had their home destroyed. The Kavilios had some neighbors, the Hardagas (a Muslim family), who gave them shelter and protection. The story goes that the Kavilios ran into Mustafa Hardaga, and he insisted that they come and seek shelter in his home. Not only did the Hardagas give asylum to the Kavilio family, they also grafted them into their family system.[39]

This is more remarkable than it may seem on the surface. Of all religious groups in the world, it is common knowledge that Muslims and Jews at best dislike one another. Within the Christian, Jewish, and Muslim worldviews, the Arab people (and by extension all Muslims) are descendants of Ishmael. For Christians and Jews, the story goes that Ishmael is cursed among men and his descendants will always live in opposition to the descendants of Isaac. With that framework in place, it is easy to interpret history simplistically, saying that the reason that Iran wants to build its nuclear program is for the purpose of destroying Israel because Iran is a Muslim nation. Since most Christians believe that they have been grafted into the family of Isaac through the death and resurrection of Jesus, they can also easily begin to see Muslims as the perpetual enemy as well.

What we learn from the story of the Kavilios and the Hardagas then is that another interpretation is possible and necessary. The Hardagas acted in loving compassion toward their literal neighbors, despite their religious differences and the traditional Isaac/Ishmael narrative. What their story requires of us is a new way of seeing past an old way of thinking.

In Palestine, Muslims and Christians fast together during Ramadan, which is the annual month of fasting for Muslims. After

---

[39] "10 Images of Jewish-Muslim Unity that Go Beyond the Headlines," *Pop Chassid*, last modified February 17, 2015, accessed July 2, 2015, http://popchassid.com/10-photos-muslim-jewish-unity/.

sixteen hours of abstaining from all food and water, they get together for Iftar (breaking the fast). This same thing happens in many cities in the United States on an annual basis.[40] In neighbor-love, one puts oneself in the shoes of the neighbor, like the Palestinian Christians and American Christians who participate in Ramadan to show solidarity and understanding across lines of difference.

Many Christians choose to believe that we cannot do anything in solidarity with Muslims. They say we have no common ground. We have no shared interests or beliefs. They are evil, and we are good. They ask, "What association does the light have with darkness?" The borders and boundaries created by our faiths have also kept others out, instead of inviting others in, it seems.

> [Solidarity] is not a feeling of vague compassion or shallow distress at the misfortunes of so many people, both near and far. On the contrary, it is a firm and persevering determination to commit oneself to the common good: that is to say, to the good of all and each individual, because we are really responsible for all...Love implies a concern for all—especially the poor—and a continued search for those social and economic structures that permit everyone to share a community that is a part of a redeemed creation.[41]

Muslims are among the most marginalized and hated groups of

---

[40] Read more about this at http://www.se7enfast.com. I started SE7EN FAST as an annual event to foster relationships between Muslim and Christian neighbors in America.

[41] "Solidarity," The United States Conference of Catholic Bishops, accessed July 23, 2015, http://www.usccb.org/beliefs-and-teachings/what-we-believe/catholic-social-teaching/solidarity.cfm.

people in America, and we can show solidarity with them as Christians because they are worth more than what our society gives to them. They are human beings made in the image of God, and therefore a show of solidarity with Muslims is a declaration that they too are human beings worthy of our concern and care, as well as our friendship. When we make the effort to put aside our biases, our clannishness, and our fear of what we don't know, we can learn new ways to love our neighbors as we love ourselves.

These stories demonstrate that sometimes loving neighbors is effortless, sometimes it is incredibly sacrificial, and sometimes it requires some creativity. Indeed, if we are to become people who believe and live out the command to love our neighbors as ourselves, something will have to change in *us* first. We will need to begin to see our neighbors as particular people whom we know and whose lives we can positively affect through the way we interact with them in loving ways on a regular basis. We can't afford to wait until our neighbors are more loveable in order to love them effectively. The first step always resides with us. We are the ones who are called to love our neighbors as we love ourselves.

Interlude

Individualism and Isolation

When it comes to peace—real, lasting, deep, and full peace—there are two primary enemies. Enemy number one is individualism. Individualism says that everyone should look out for number one, namely him- or herself. Individualism reigns supreme in most of the Western world. The problem with individualism is that it negates human nature. We were created to be in community with one another. Communities look out for the interests of a community, not individuals. The same can be said about loving our neighbors as we love ourselves. We love when we act concretely on behalf of those whom we call neighbors, out of compassion and a desire for their well-being. When we view things primarily as *mine* rather than *ours*, we are denying part of our nature as human beings. As John Donne famously wrote,

> No man is an island,
> Entire of itself;
> Every man is a piece of the continent,
> A part of the main.

> Any man's death diminishes me,
> Because I am involved in mankind,
> And therefore never send to know for whom the bell tolls;
> It tolls for thee.[42]

---

[42] "No Man Is an Island," *Poetry*, accessed September 29, 2015, https://web.cs.dal.ca/~johnston/poetry/island.html.

A woman named Deb, a Jew living in Israel, sees this as the main cause of the tension between Israel and Palestine. She says,

> I think that we have to understand human rights today as interactive; it can't be about "I worry about my human rights, you worry about yours." That doesn't work anymore. The basic human right we need today is the right not to be enemies, the right to refuse to slaughter each other. We can't actualize this right by ourselves, we need others to do it with us.[43]

"The basic human right we need today is the right not to be enemies." Let that statement sink in for a moment. I am to worry about the rights of all people, not just my own individual rights, and not just to worry about them, but also to engage in creating spaces for those rights to be had by all. Peace requires community, not individualism.

Enemy number two of peace is isolation. This is yet another problem in Western culture. We rarely know the people who live next door. When my wife and I lived in our first house, the neighbors across the street, whose house was an eerie gray color, never came outside. We also never made the effort to meet them. In fact, one year for Christmas, we made cookies for all of the neighbors and delivered them door to door. We skipped the creepy house across the street. We justified this exclusion (or should we say isolation) by convincing ourselves that they would probably try to shoot us if we

---

[43] "Magazine: Meet Israel's Boycotters," *Al Jazeera English*, last modified June 8, 2015, accessed September 29, 2015, http://www.aljazeera.com/indepth/features/2015/05/magazine-meet-israel-boycotters-150528072013581.html.

knocked on their door. When we don't know the people we live near, we are able to make up all sorts of stories and histories about them that make them into whatever sort of creepy, monstrous, or idiosyncratic people we imagine them to be. This lack of true knowledge leads to fear, which almost always leads to hatred.

Another Israeli, named Haggai, has this to say about the barriers to peace between his people and the Palestinians:

> What the separation has done—with its walls and laws and checkpoints—is make it easier for one side to demonize and dehumanize the other. So, younger people here have probably never even met Palestinians, unless it was while they were in the army when they are in a fighting situation. And it's the same on the other side. That makes it much easier for Israelis to say that all of the Palestinians are monsters and terrorists and for the Palestinians to say that all of the Israelis are killers. It's a very basic matter of human contact.[44]

Isolation works against peace on both sides of the isolation. Whether I am actively isolating my neighbor or my enemy or I am the neighbor or enemy who is being isolated, peace is next to impossible between us. This, again, goes back to our basic human nature. When we live in community with the people in our own neighborhood, we prevent ourselves from becoming hateful and fearful of those around us. When we live in community rather than isolation, we can live at peace.

---

[44] Ibid.

It's easy to project the need for peace on the seemingly endless conflict between Israel and Palestine. It's not as easy when we look at our own way of being in the world—how we choose to act for our own benefit over or against others and how we isolate ourselves from others and others from ourselves. If we are to be for peace, we have to be *for community*. Just as it wasn't good for man to be alone, it is no good for any of us to be alone. When we know our neighbors, when we make neighbors out of strangers and enemies, we are creating an open space for peace to break out.

3
Strangers

The alien who resides with you shall be to you as the citizen among you; you shall love the alien as yourself, for you were aliens in the land of Egypt: I am the LORD your God.

- Leviticus 19:34 (NRSV).

Come…inherit the kingdom prepared for you from the foundation of the world; for I was hungry and you gave me food, I was thirsty and you gave me something to drink, I was a stranger and you welcomed me, I was naked and you gave me clothing, I was sick and you took care of me, I was in prison and you visited me. - Matthew 25:34–5 (NRSV).

Mutual Fear

Any good parent knows that one of the first and most important lessons you can teach your children is don't talk to strangers. Urban legends abound of a man in a dark sedan who pulls up to the sidewalk and asks a young child, "Do you want a lollipop?" The child, of course, *wants* a lollipop, so he or she unwittingly gets into the car with the stranger and disappears without a trace. Child abductions are real and serious, and our culture has made an industry out of retelling this tale in cinema, television, and books—making heroes out of ordinary people who rescue the abducted child from the clutches of the sinister kidnapper.

Consider the signs on the Interstate that advise us not to stop for hitchhikers while passing a federal prison. The natural conclusion for all of us is to consider *every* hitchhiker, every person stranded on the side of the road, and perhaps every stranger as a potential threat to our safety. This narrative has one primary point: *beware of everyone you don't know*.

So, instinctively, in certain strange neighborhoods, you find yourself locking the car doors at a stoplight. For some reason, you feel unsafe, despite the fact that other people here are safely walking on the sidewalk. Perhaps it is the way people look or the way people are dressed. Whatever the reason, you perceive some sort of danger if you don't protect yourself from those outside your car. Not only do you see the people outside of your car as potentially dangerous

74

strangers, you also recognize yourself as a stranger in a strange place. With the push of a button, you lend credence to the narrative that the stranger is to be feared and also that the stranger should be afraid.

I don't want to minimize this fear. For most of us, the fear of strangers is a natural outcome of what we learned as children about others. Indeed, it may even be completely natural to what it means to be a human. However, I am not convinced that fear of strangers leads to safety or that living without fear leads one into dangerous situations. Anyone who has spent any time living in a strange place, be it a strange neighborhood or a foreign country, will tell you that the people who are most in danger are the ones who look like they *think* they are in danger. When I lived in Jordan, I could easily tell the difference between a tourist and someone who lived in Jordan simply by the look on the person's face. When we first arrived in Jordan, many taxi drivers took advantage of us because we had that look. We looked like we didn't feel safe, like we didn't belong, and because of it, we were vulnerable.

My wife and I took a trip to Aqaba (the Red Sea port in Jordan) early in our journey to Jordan, armed only with our Lonely Planet guide and our ever-present sense of adventure. We got off of the bus and hailed a taxi. I told the taxi driver we wanted to go to the Dweek One Hotel, which was a couple of blocks from the bus station. Sensing we were strangers, the taxi driver proceeded to drive us several miles outside of town to a remote beach near the border of

Saudi Arabia. As he drove, my fear radar increased dramatically. I had no idea what this guy was about to do. When he parked at the beach, he told us we could get out, relax, and enjoy the beach, and he would stay in the parking lot to drive us to our hotel. He saw us as wealthy tourists when in fact we were only poor volunteers. I told the driver that we weren't interested in going to this beach and asked him if he would please take us to our hotel.

He was furious, but he held it together. I was also furious, because I thought we had moved past the point of being strangers in a strange land. I was angry with him for thinking that he could take advantage of us. When he pulled up to the Dweek One Hotel, he pointed to his meter and said it would be 10 JD (about $15). I pulled out 1 JD from my wallet and firmly explained to him that he had taken us only a few blocks from where we started, so I would give him what he should have been paid if he had simply done what we had asked. He yelled. I yelled. I threw the dinar onto the seat and slammed the door (not one of my finer moments). His tires screeched as he drove off, and I spent the rest of the trip to Aqaba as a stranger, looking over my shoulder for that driver, who I feared might exact his revenge at any moment. We were unsafe on that trip precisely because we looked like strangers. Later, once we believed that we belonged in our neighborhood and in this foreign country, we started looking like neighbors rather than strangers. We were safe when we were no longer strangers.

When we returned home, we got an apartment in a very diverse area of downtown Peoria, Illinois. People would often ask us, "Don't you feel unsafe in that neighborhood?" The answer was always no. I had learned in Jordan that I am only as unsafe as I perceive myself to be. When I act like I belong, I no longer make myself a stranger and I also no longer treat everyone else that way.

While it is patently false that parents should not teach their children not to talk to strangers, how does this narrative play out as we enter into adulthood? Does that advice serve to help us find safety as we move through life? To what extent does this increase our divisions, decrease our sense of neighborliness, and keep us content to simply love and interact with the people we know? Is this fear of the stranger good or bad for society?

As I wrote that last paragraph, a man named Tyler came to our door selling security and safety (his timing was impeccable). He noticed that we didn't have a sign in our yard, displaying to the neighbors that they shouldn't try to break in. He wanted us to be protected by whatever home security he was selling. The problem with the companies like the one Tyler works for is that they aren't selling safety at all. These companies sell the *illusion* of safety. They sell the idea that as long as you have a sign in your front lawn, no one can break into your house and steal your kids or your things. Safety can't be bought or sold with a sign that tells strangers to "Keep Out!" Safety really isn't a guarantee for any of us. I believe and have experienced that the only true hope we have to live safely in our homes and communities is for us to live in loving ways toward strangers, turning them into neighbors and friends, rather than isolating ourselves into our fortified enclaves we call our homes.[45]

Stranger Love

In the previous chapter, we looked at how Leviticus 19 is the pinnacle of the pinnacle of the Torah.[46] Much has been said and written about the command, "You shall love your neighbor as yourselves." It is a command that is held in high regard by Muslims, Jews, and Christians. Far less has been said or written about the command in Leviticus 19:34: "The alien who resides with you shall be to you as the citizen among you; *you shall love the alien as yourself,* for you were aliens in the land of Egypt: I am the LORD your God." It is worth noting that this command is found in close proximity to its partner command in 19:18, in the pivotal and ever-important chapter on holy living in community. In an oral culture like that of ancient Israel, the mention of the well-known command to love our neighbors would cause its hearers to recite or remember the verses that surround it. This command to love strangers as ourselves, found only sixteen short verses from the greatest commandment, was ever on the minds and tongues of the ancient Israelites. For this reason, I believe that the command to love

---

[45] If you have a home security system, please don't be offended and please keep reading. I understand that there are myriad reasons why people purchase home security systems, from past negative experiences to general fear of the unknown, or even as a requirement by an HOA. My point here is simply that we can't buy safety; we can only work to create safety through the way we live toward others in our communities.

[46] With 19:18 being the pinnacle of the pinnacle of the pinnacle of the Torah.

strangers as ourselves can serve as a helpful corrective to any minimizing of the command to love our neighbors. This command has a certain universalizing effect on our understanding of the previous one.

Who were the "aliens" who resided within Israel, whom Israel was called to love like neighbors, and who helped them to recall their own tragic history as "aliens" in Egypt? First, it would be helpful for us to understand the meaning of the word *alien* as it is used in Hebrew—*ger*. A *ger* is literally a sojourner, and the word is translated as *foreigner, immigrant, alien,* and *stranger* in the Old Testament and Torah. Rabbi Arik Ascherman points out, "The most repeated commandment in the Torah is to love the *ger* (stranger), and not to oppress him or her."[47] Of the 613 commandments found in the Old Testament, up to forty-six are related to the correct and just treatment of strangers.

Some interpreters of the Torah have taken the "stranger" to mean a foreigner who has converted to Judaism.[48] If that were the case, then the commandment would be much easier to follow. *Love your neighbor* (your fellow ethnic Jew) and *love the stranger* (your fellow convert to Judaism) mean essentially the same thing in this case: love your fellow Jews to the potential exclusion of everyone else. Indeed, in ancient and modern times, we have seen that this

---

[47] Kelly James Clark, ed., *Abraham's Children: Liberty and Tolerance in an Age of Religious Conflict* (New Haven: Yale University Press, 2012), 89.
[48] Ibid.

interpretation has allowed for Israel to mistreat strangers because they themselves aren't Jews.

To the contrary, Ascherman argues that this interpretation doesn't hold weight. "[The] justification for this oft-repeated commandment is that we were strangers in the land of Egypt. Unless Jews had converted to the Egyptian religion, the *ger toshav* is the 'other' in our midst who agrees to abide by the basic rules of our society."[49] What Ascherman is saying is if the argument is made that the stranger is a convert to Judaism, we must assume that the Jews converted to the Egyptian religion while they were enslaved in Egypt, since the same word is used of the Israelites in the rationale for the command. We also know that this is not the case. Therefore one cannot justifiably argue that the stranger is a convert from one religious system to another. The "basic rules" referred to by Ascherman are what Jews refer to as the Noahide commandments. These are rules against murder, idolatry, sexual immorality, and theft, for instance. "Although our tradition does not expect all people to observe the many commandments incumbent on Jews, we are not relativists. We believe that all humanity should observe these…fundamental principles."[50] As long as the non-Jew strangers live according to certain universal moral standards, Jews are commanded to love them and treat them with justice, dignity, and respect, according to him.

---

[49] Ibid.
[50] Ibid., 82.

Even this is open to interpretation, however. In 2015, a Catholic church in Israel was set on fire because of the apparent belief that Christians are idolaters. Spray-painted on the walls of the church, in Hebrew, was the phrase "the idolaters shall be cast out."[51] It seems that, in the arsonists' interpretation of the Noahide commandments, Christians *can* be considered in violation of these "basic rules" and therefore not be protected. It is important to bear in mind as we continue to consider the meaning of the commands to love neighbors, strangers, and enemies that all we are doing is *interpreting* meaning. Unfortunately, there is no one correct way to interpret scripture; we are simply giving it our best shot.

Perhaps the best way for us to understand the meaning of the command to love strangers as we love ourselves in Leviticus 19:34 is to understand the rationale given for the command. "[For] you were aliens in the land of Egypt." For four hundred years (more or less), the Israelites were made to be slaves in the land of Egypt. As slaves, the Israelites had to bake the bricks used in building Pharaoh's buildings. Things got so bad that, at one point, Pharaoh was even forcing the slaves to collect the straw they needed to bake bricks for building, while still keeping up the same quantity of work. By the time Israel got away from this oppression, they had almost completely forgotten what it meant to be human beings living among

---

[51] "Catholic Church in Israel Badly Damaged by Suspected Arson Attack," *Guardian*, last modified June 18, 2015, accessed June 29, 2015, http://www.theguardian.com/world/2015/jun/18/catholic-church-multiplication-israel-damaged-possible-arson-attack.

other human beings. They had been stripped of their humanity, as their only reality had been the brutality of slavery for ten or more generations. The Torah, then, was God's way of making this newly formed nation into a society unlike that of Egypt. They needed a new model, a new way of being in the world so that they would not go the way of Pharaoh in their newfound freedom.

> Therefore beware, so runs the warning, from making rights in our own state conditional on anything other than on basic humanity, which dwells in every human by virtue of being human. With any suppression of these human rights the gate is open to the brazen mistreatment of other humans. This is the root of the Egyptian horror.[52]

Rabbi Samson Hirsch, quoted above, believed that it is so important for Jews to remember what happened in Egypt "because our own experiences do not make us immune to Pharaoh residing in our hearts."[53] When oppression has been the norm, it is easy to fall into a pattern in which the victim begins to victimize others. This is one reason why the command to love the non-Jew foreigner is so important. Love does not oppress or enslave the other.

Today, the need for remembrance of past oppression has never been greater. According to the United Nations High Commissioner for Refugees (UNHCR), at the end of 2015, there were over eleven million people who were considered to be refugees in our world, with over four million from war-affected areas in the Middle East

---

[52] Clark, *Abraham's Children*, 91.
[53] Clark, *Abraham's Children*, 91.

and Southwest Asia.[54] If we forget our past oppression, whether it is the slavery of the Israelites in Egypt, the persecution of the early church, the Holocaust, or the current oppression of Muslim populations in various places in the Middle East, we can easily succumb to the voices in our culture that tell us to keep those seeking asylum out of our countries. When we do this, we become complicit in the oppression of refugees. When we do this, we submit to the Pharaohs residing in our own hearts. Never has there been a more relevant command than to love strangers as we love ourselves. As people who all have a history of being on the receiving end of oppression, we cannot afford to forget our own histories or to isolate ourselves from strangers.

You're a *Dhimmi*

In Islam, there are particular provisions made for people of the book (Jews and Christians), also known as *dhimmi*, who live under the rule of an Islamic nation. Islam has long emphasized that there can be no compulsion in religion, and the laws regarding how dhimmi are to be treated are related to this pluralistic religious outlook. Much of this plurality and tolerance is due to the history of Islam in the time of the Prophet Muhammad.

As has been noted previously, the Prophet Muhammad emigrated to Yathrib (Medina), a loosely knit conglomeration of

---

[54] "Figures at a Glance," UNHCR, accessed January, 21, 2016, http://www.unhcr.org/pages/49c3646c11.html.

many Jewish tribes. It was in Yathrib that the Prophet Muhammad revealed that the Torah, the Gospels, and the Qur'an are contained in a heavenly book called *Umm al-Kitab* (or the "Mother of Books").

> Muhammad may have understood the concept of the *Umm al-Kitab* to mean not only that the Jews, Christians, and Muslims shared a single divine scripture but also that they constituted a single divine *Ummah*[55]...Muhammad aligned his community with the Jews in Medina because he considered them, as well as the Christians, to be part of his Ummah. Consequently, when he came to Medina, he made Jerusalem—the site of the Temple (long since destroyed) and the direction in which the Diaspora Jews turned during worship—the direction of prayer, or *qiblah*, for all Muslims. He imposed a mandatory fast upon his community which was to take place annually on the tenth day (*Ashura*) of the first month of the Jewish calendar, the day more commonly known as Yom Kippur. He purposely set the day of Muslim congregation at noon on Friday so that it would coincide with, but not disrupt, Jewish preparation for the Sabbath.[56]

The Prophet Muhammad indeed seemed to exemplify the importance of loving strangers, or at least treating strangers with respect in the way he treated the Jews in Yathrib. In light of this, it is no wonder that there developed laws in sharia regarding the treatment of dhimmi in Islamic lands.

---

[55] *Ummah* means family or tribe.
[56] Reza Aslan, *No God but God: The Origins, Evolution, and Future of Islam* (New York: Random House, 2006), 99–100. Aslan is writing here against the traditional belief that there was an underlying anti-Semitism within early Islam. His is only one perspective among many on this issue.

Essentially, dhimmi were allowed under Islamic law to continue to practice their religion and, in some cases, even to have their own governing authority.[57] This wasn't a free gift, however. A tax, called *jizyah*, was levied on dhimmi who did not convert to Islam when the Islamic empire expanded into their territory. The options for dhimmi seem to have been that either they could convert to Islam (and avoid the jizyah), they could move out of the Muslim-controlled territory, or they could pay jizyah and continue to live in their land and practice their religion. In return for the jizyah, Christians and Jews under Islamic rule were *free* to practice their religion. We have seen the same sort of attitude toward dhimmi most recently in the lands controlled by ISIS.[58] Despite all of the fear that ISIS inflicted upon the global community, they followed the dhimmi laws by giving the same options to Christians living in the lands under their control in Syria and Iraq: convert, leave, or pay *jizyah*.

"[Dhimmi] were not, however, tolerated in the sense of being regarded as equals. *Dhimmi* had a separate and clearly subordinate social and legal status...Christians, for example, were not allowed to ring church bells."[59] In addition to the law against ringing church

---

[57] Aslan, *No God but God*, 94.

[58] As barbaric as it seems, there is only one aspect of ISIS in relation to dhimmi that runs contrary to these laws. There are plenty of reports of Christians being executed by members of ISIS. This is not sanctioned either by sharia or the Qur'an. The Prophet Muhammad warned that he would stand against any Muslim who even wrongs a Jew or a Christian on Judgment Day. This is a little-known fact, but is worth noting.

[59] Jessica A. Coope, "Religious and Cultural Conversion to Islam in Ninth-Century Umayyad Cordoba," *Journal of World History* 4, no. 1 (Spring 1993): 50.

bells (which feels rather arbitrary), dhimmi were required to dress distinctly from Muslims. I learned in the first few weeks while living in Jordan that this is still an important cultural motif, at least among Christians there. When I moved to Jordan, I had a five-month-old beard (which, for me, was substantial). I was told by Kamal, a Christian companion, that "Christians don't have beards." I didn't know what to do with this information, so for no apparent reason, I shaved off my mustache (admittedly, this makes no sense). The next day, I learned from other Christians that a beard with no mustache is a sign in Jordan of being a fundamentalist or radical Muslim, since this was the traditional way Muhammad had worn his beard. Not wanting to associate myself with radical Islam, I shaved off my beard completely and subsequently looked like a twelve-year-old prepubescent boy. I eventually gave up on this cultural conundrum altogether, and grew back my beard in force.

In an attempt to normalize this reality in the Muslim world, it might be helpful to craft an analogy about the democratic ideal of the separation of church and state in the United States. We are given the freedom to practice our religion so far as the free practice of our religion doesn't violate democratic values, the laws of the nation, or the laws of the state. The same could be said of the laws of *dhimmitude* in Islamic societies. A Christian or a Jew is free to practice his or her religion so far as the practice doesn't violate the Islamic ideals and laws of the Islamic state.

Dhimmi, to this day, are not allowed to proselytize their faith to Muslims in most Islamic societies.[60] This, according to Reza Aslan, could be one explanation for why Christianity has all but disappeared in much of the Muslim world.[61] It is still a contested question as to what the status of dhimmi in Islamic countries is. We might not be able to qualify whether they are treated tolerably or not. Regardless, Islamic law has always provided for the protection of dhimmi, as strangers living among them. Though we cannot say that strangers are to be *loved* in the same way as neighbors in Islam, we can say that there were provisions made for strangers (at least Jews and Christians) to practice their religion and remain living in Muslim lands through the course of history.

Good Samaritans?

Samaritans were the quintessential stranger-enemies of Israel. The conflict between the Samaritans and the Jews was more than religious. The Jews worshipped in Jerusalem, and the Samaritans worshipped on Mount Gerazim. The Samaritans were like second cousins to the Jews, sharing many worship rituals and sharing the same Torah. I have heard it said that when the Romans came into Palestine in conquest, the Samaritans denied that there were any Jews living in the land, which led to much of the animosity between the two groups.[62] Jewish tradition regarded the Samaritans as a

---

[60] Hence the discomfort I felt during my conversation with Jamal in chapter 1.

[61] Aslan, *No God but God*, 95.

[62] I must note that this is anecdotal. I was unable to verify this story with any documented evidence. Regardless, if true, it makes for an understandable reason for some of the conflict between Jews and Samaritans historically.

mixed-race, polytheistic group of people, and as such, they were in violation of the Noahide commandments mentioned earlier.[63] So, when Jesus and his disciples were not welcomed by the Samaritans in Luke's gospel, it is no surprise that the disciples asked Jesus if he wanted them to call down fire from heaven to destroy them; they were strangers, and they were enemies.[64]

Within this context, Jesus told a parable of a *good* Samaritan. This unnamed Samaritan showed compassion toward a stranger in need, more than the holiest men of Israel. It is easy to imagine how incongruous this parable must have sounded to Jesus's fellow Jews. Jesus had a penchant for crafting stories that flipped every social norm on its head. Much, perhaps too much, has been made of this parable. Hospitals have been named after this anonymous and fictional character, people have been praised for being "good Samaritans," and people have been equally cursed for the same, albeit sarcastic, reason.

What *is* worth noting, however, is that Jesus told this well-known parable in response to the question "And who is my neighbor?" Instead of answering the question, he told the story of a stranger acting neighborly toward a Jew. This stranger helped a stranger like a neighbor helps a neighbor.

The parable does not actually explain who qualifies as a

---

[63] John P. Meier, "The Historical Jesus and the Historical Samaritans: What Can Be Said?," *Biblica* 81, no. 2 (2000): 214.
[64] Luke 9:51–55 (NRSV).

neighbor. Instead, it displays what it means to be a loving neighbor toward any fellow human being in need. Strictly speaking, Jesus did not answer the scribe's question. He reconstructed that question in a manner that emphasizes our agency as persons. Then, he summons us to exemplify authentic agape toward any and all of our fellow human beings regardless of their existing beliefs and commitments.[65]

In essence, Jesus interpreted the command to love neighbors in light of the command to love strangers. Since Samaritans were non-Jews, they were strangers who lived in the midst of occupied Israel (under Rome). As such, rather than treat them as second-class citizens and oppress them, they were to love them as if they were neighbors. It's a remarkable parable, not only for its countercultural challenge, but also for the way in which Jesus used it to point to both of the commands to love neighbors and to love strangers as we love ourselves.

It is also worth noting the response of the lawyer to Jesus's parable about the good Samaritan. Jesus asked, rhetorically, "'Which of these three, do you think, was a neighbor to the man who fell into the hands of the robbers?' He [the lawyer] said, 'The one who showed him mercy.' Jesus said to him, 'Go and do likewise.'"[66] Unwilling to say "the Samaritan," the lawyer gave an ambiguous response as to who was the neighbor in the parable. It was too difficult for him to admit that it was a Samaritan, as opposed to a priest and a Levite,

---

[65] Thomas W. Ogletree, "The Essential Unity of the Love Commands: Moving Beyond Paradox," *The Journal of Religious Ethics* 35, no. 4 (Dec. 2007): 698–699.
[66] Luke 10:36–37 (NRSV).

who was the hero and the example. His ambiguous answer serves to reinforce the point that Jews really took issue with the Samaritans. However, he did not simply ignore the ethnic and religious background of the hero of the story. His answer also reveals that love is demonstrated in compassionate action on behalf of the other. Jesus didn't tell the lawyer to go and become a Samaritan. That would be sacrilegious and antithetical to the point of the story. Rather, he told the lawyer to go and love the stranger and neighbor through acts of compassion and mercy. This is the essence of the dual commands of loving neighbor and stranger.

I think that we might benefit from putting the Samaritan into some different religious or cultural clothes. If Jesus were in Israel-Palestine today, a story of a Good Samaritan wouldn't bear as much weight. Who are the religious half-cousins of the Jews? Christians and Muslims. Who are the religious half-cousins of Muslims? Jews and Christians. Who are the religious half-cousins of Christians? Jews and Muslims. So, in Israel today, Jesus would likely have told the story of the good Palestinian, the good Arab, or the good Muslim (and in some cases the good Christian). In Palestine, the story would be that of the good Israeli or the good Jew (and again, the good Christian). In America, to Christians, the story would almost certainly be about the good Muslim. The parallels are too clear to miss, aren't they? I believe this is why this story remains incredibly relevant to our discussions about strangers and how they are to be treated. Jesus wasn't just telling a story for those people then, but for us, now, if we have ears to hear.

Strangers in Strange Places

Most of us have had the experience of being a stranger in a strange place—whether at a party where we didn't know anyone or in a foreign country where we stuck out like an orange in a bushel of apples. For white American Christians, it may be difficult for us to remember moments when we were considered strange. But if we are honest, we can certainly think of a time when we sensed the eyes of everyone in the room looking at us as if we didn't belong. It is a healthy exercise to put ourselves in these types of situations, especially if we want to learn how we can love strangers as we love ourselves.

My most recent experience of this was at a McDonald's in Utah County, Utah. I had a large beard and (still have) more than my share of tattoos, so in a conservative and ultra-Mormon place like Utah County, I was clearly a stranger.[67] Sure enough, two minivan-driving moms rubbernecked as I walked into the restaurant, and an old man almost tripped and fell on account of staring at me. I didn't belong, and their looks of suspicion toward me confirmed that. When we are able to remember what it feels like to be a stranger in a strange place, we can more easily think of ways we can welcome and love strangers when we encounter them—even if it's as simple as saying hello.

---

[67] Utah County is 98 percent Mormon. I don't look the part.

You might think that saying hello is too simplistic, that loving strangers certainly entails much more than that. And sometimes it might but not always. A few years ago, our family was grocery shopping at the local Shop 'N' Save. As we passed the canned food aisle, I noticed a woman in hijab and burka browsing the garbanzo beans, so I told my wife that she should go say hello to the woman. Our time in Jordan has made us ultra-aware of Muslims wherever we go. She objected at first, mostly because of the whole cultural convention we have in America to ignore strangers and just go about our business.

I eventually convinced her to greet the woman, and as I pushed the kids in the cart, my wife went up to her and said, "As salaamu alaykum," the traditional Arabic greeting that we learned while living in Jordan. My wife extended a welcoming hand to this stranger, whose name we found out was Fatima. Fatima said she worked at the local Islamic school in our town and was planning out the meal she would make for her family to break fast, as it was Ramadan. Pretty unremarkable stuff, right?

That's not the end of the story, however. About a month later, my wife started a three-month stint as a substitute teacher at the Islamic school where Fatima worked. Now, instead of simply being the nice, white Christian woman who worked at the Islamic school, to Fatima, my wife was now the nice, white Christian woman who worked at the Islamic school and also said hello to her at the grocery store when she was nothing but a stranger. The simple act of saying hello changed the context of their relationship forever. We never know when we will be in contact with the strangers that we meet randomly at the grocery store. The way we treat them can go a long way toward changing the context of any potential future relationship we might have with the strangers in our midst.

More recently, I was on a train in Denver with my brother. We had just finished watching a baseball game and were returning to the house where we were staying. I noticed two guys speaking in Arabic to one another a few rows ahead of us. Having lived in the Middle East, I found their chatter a welcome sound, as I had learned enough Arabic while living in Jordan to carry on a very basic conversation. There was a man standing near these two young men who himself was noticeably uncomfortable. I imagined his discomfort was due to the fear that these two Arabic-speaking guys were up to no good, or perhaps that they were potential terrorists on public transportation.

When the train stopped at a station, he moved to a different location in the car. I took the opportunity to move closer to these guys and interrupted their conversation in Arabic, saying, "Do you speak Arabic?"[68] They looked confused and answered in the affirmative. We began talking, now in English, and I learned that they were students at the University of Denver, learning English in order to return to Saudi Arabia (their home country) to complete

---

[68] This is one of my favorite things to do, simply because it is incredibly confusing to be interrupted in your own language by someone asking if you are speaking the language you are clearly speaking.

their university degrees. They then told me that I was the first American who had talked to them in six months of living in America. I was astonished and frustrated. How could these two live in my country for six months and never be acknowledged or approached by another American? What sort of message does that give to them about America or Christianity?

This takes me back to the guy who was uncomfortable in the presence of these strangers. If his discomfort was based in fear, however rational, he allowed that fear to take root in him. Maybe he got off the train and later told his wife that there were two suspicious Arabs on the train. Maybe he saw me talking to them and began to wonder what was wrong with me or if I was in on their plot to take over America. Maybe he thought nothing at all. On the flip side, perhaps he saw me walk up to these young men and, without fear, engage them in conversation and then realized how unfounded his fear of them had been. We will never know.

My brother and I had had some difficult conversations earlier that day about my work and my desire to help the Church move past fear and into love in relation to Muslims in our communities. When we got off the train, however, he said, "I can see what you're talking about now. What you're doing is pretty important." Whether or not the anonymous man on the train felt that same wash of realization, my brother did. A lot can be said for living without fear alongside those who aren't there yet.

We are told that we fear what we don't know or understand. Instead of taking the chance and seeking to get to know these young men, to understand their story, and having a story to tell of the strangers on the train who were just two normal guys trying to make a better life for themselves, he chose to move to another part of the train. He chose the way of fear instead of the way of love. Admittedly, it's the path we often take. I believe he missed out on something special that night, which is the opportunity to change the minds of these two strangers about America and to change himself into a more open and loving person toward strangers in the future.

Example and Counterexample

HRH Prince Ghazi bin Muhammad was a student just like the two guys on the train in Denver. Before becoming the chief advisor for religious and cultural affairs for the country of Jordan and the author of the *Common Word* document, he was once just a foreign student from a Muslim country on an American university campus. His cousin, HRH King Abdullah II of Jordan, was also once just a stranger on campus at Georgetown University. King Abdullah II is now sponsoring a research program at one of his alma maters, Oxford, which will be focused on researching the concept of love in the religions of Islam and Christianity (sounds familiar). Two of the most influential men in terms of creating bridges between Muslims, Christians, *and* Jews at one time were in the same situation as the students from Denver—sojourners, strangers, and aliens.

When I think about HRH Prince Ghazi and HRH King Abdullah, I wonder about what their experience was like on campus in America. Were they as isolated from the broader culture as the guys I met on the train? Were they treated with love or with suspicion? My hunch is, given their current status as consummate bridge-builders, they had a positive experience not only with American culture but also with Christianity. Ghazi has written, "If Muslims and Christians are not at peace, the world cannot be at peace."[69] One cannot believe in or work for peace if one has not seen that peace is possible through relationships across lines of difference.

It would be easy to dismiss these stories given that the King and the Prince were students at a much different time than the one we are in today. The events of September 11, 2001, have radically changed American culture. As true as that may be, Sayyid Qutb's story serves as a cautionary tale and a counterexample to that of HRH Prince Ghazi and HRH King Abdullah. Qutb attended the University of Northern Colorado in the mid-twentieth century prior to becoming one of the theological inspirations for the Muslim Brotherhood. The Muslim Brotherhood is a political party committed to social reforms (among other things) in the Muslim world. Of these reforms, some are clearly a reaction against cultural imperialism exported by the United States into the Muslim world. Many of the Brotherhood's social reforms are related to the way women dress, how women should act, keeping male and female students segregated

---

[69] Volf, *A Common Word*, 49.

in the classroom, making private meetings between men and women illegal, and closing undesirable social clubs.[70] The Brotherhood has also spawned such terrorist organizations as Hamas and Islamic Jihad. It would seem that Qutb's experience on campus, by inference, was less than positive. He was just a student on campus, like the King, the Prince, and the two Saudi students, at a much more peaceful time in history. But we could justifiably assume that his experience in America resulted in a reaction against all things culturally American, which he then codified into a systematic anti-imperialist, anti-American set of teachings and writings.

Another young Muslim man, Tamerlan Tsarnaev, lived for five years in the United States in the city of Boston. He was a boxer and a talented one at that. He had hopes to make the US Olympic boxing team and was training vigorously toward that end. In a photo essay entitled "Will Box for Passport," he was quoted as saying, "I don't have a single American friend. I don't understand them." Three years later, Tamerlan and his brother Dzokhar carried out the Boston Marathon bombing, taking the lives of three people and injuring hundreds of others.[71]

---

[70] Nancy J. Davis and Robert V. Robinson, "Overcoming Movement Obstacles by the Religiously Orthodox: The Muslim Brotherhood in Egypt, the Shas in Israel, Comunione e Liberazione in Italy, and the Salvation Army in the United States," *American Journal of Sociology* 114, no. 5 (March 2009): 1304.

[71] "'I Don't Have a Single American Friend': Photo Essay Titled 'Will Box for Passport' Reveals Profile of Boston Bombing Suspect Tamerlan Tsarnaev," *Independent*, last modified April 19, 2013, accessed July 7, 2015, http://www.independent.co.uk/news/world/americas/i-dont-have-a-single-american-friend-photo-essay-titled-will-box-for-passport-reveals-profile-of-boston-bombing-suspect-tamerlan-tsarnaev-8580575.html.

Though Tamerlan's comment could be considered hyperbole, it is nonetheless instructive. I can't keep myself from imagining a different outcome for him. If he *did* have a friend, even one person, who chose to love him like he or she loved him- or herself (despite his status as a stranger), would he have carried out the heinous attack? Would he have risked the life of a friend in order to send whatever message he was trying to send? I like to think otherwise.

One of the contributing factors to extremism and terrorism, whether religiously motivated or not, is isolation from the broader culture. This is why engaging in relationships with strangers across lines of cultural, ethnic, or religious difference is so vitally important today. If Tamerlan had had a friend who was a Christian or simply an American, he would have also had a human filter for information through that friendship. One of the important parts about being in relationships with strangers (who, by default, are no longer strangers) is that we can ask them if what we see in the media is actually true of them or their way of seeing the world. If Tamerlan had had that sort of a relationship, I believe it would have been much more difficult for him to make the decision to do what he ultimately did. Perhaps love could have even prevented it altogether.

One could argue that there are many other factors that led to Sayyid Qutb's desire for social reform in Egypt and Tamerlan Tsarnaev's decision to carry out a terrorist attack in Boston. Psychological and sociological factors aside, the argument I am making is that the only sure way in which we can change the narrative and transform strangers among us into friends and neighbors is to actively and concretely love them. *Love is not a hopeless endeavor.* Rather, love is the antidote, the variable in the relational equation that has the chance of making a better world in the future. Tamerlan's story reminds us that strangers can easily become enemies without people in their lives who choose to love them and engage in life-changing, life-giving relationships across lines of difference. HRH King Abdullah II and HRH Prince Ghazi remind us that another future is possible, if we will only take the risk.

There are hundreds of thousands of students from the Middle East and North Africa studying on American campuses today. The potential that future world-changers, for better or worse, are living and studying on our local campuses today is quite high. These students will return home with not only a book education but a cultural education as well. Will the way we interact with these strangers lead these students to return home seeking to make pathways toward peace between Islam and Christianity? Or, like Qutb, will we inspire these students toward disdain, hatred, or potential violence? No one knows for sure. *The only thing we can control is how we treat strangers among us.* May we choose to love the stranger as we love ourselves, through the pursuit of knowledge and understanding their stories, and transform the stranger into a neighbor and friend in the process. The future of our world just might depend on it.

Interlude

The Fourth of July

Our family visited my wife's grandmother at the assisted-living facility where she resides on the day before Independence Day. She has a steady feed of Fox News running in her living room at all times. On this particular day, the big buzz in the twenty-four-hour news cycle was the threat of a terror attack in major cities in the United States on the Fourth of July. She was clearly worried about it, after having been pummeled over the head by this misinformation for the past however many hours.

I had not heard anything about this news, so when I arrived home that day, I did a cursory search for any reliable news source covering this story. ABC, CNN, Fox, NBC, neo-conservative, and conservative websites showed up, all carrying the story. Strikingly absent was any such story on the BBC, the *Atlantic*, the *Guardian*, NPR, Al Jazeera (English, not America), or any other relatively neutral website (related to this sort of a story). I shrugged my shoulders and decided that there wasn't anything to worry about. After all, our major news outlets in America are basically in the same business: What's the biggest, scariest news story, and how can we exploit it to make ratings go up?

So, what can we learn about the nothing that happened that day in comparison to the something that was made of it by our major news media?

We could say that the date was too obvious; never has a major terror attack in a Western country made logical sense (no matter how much you want to make of Qur'an 9:111[72]). Terror is almost always random. That's what is terrifying about it. It also gains traction when we are made to be afraid of things happening on major holidays. Terrorism reigns supreme when an entire country is afraid of an attack on the Fourth of July. Terrorists don't have to attack on obvious days because we are already afraid on those days. Even though nothing happened on that particular Independence Day, it might as well have. We were already victimized by our own fear (and our media).

The same sort of fear has reinforced our airways and airports with heightened security measures and had us expecting violence to break out at a "Bikers against Islam" rally in Phoenix. CNN was reporting on this particular day that new plans for Prophet Muhammad cartoon contests could incite more terrorist attacks. Terrorism isn't protest. Terrorism seeks to exact the maximum amount of fear on the maximum number of people. When terrorism

---

[72] I have heard my fair share of Christian apologists point to Qur'an 9:111 as the reason for the date of the attacks on September 11, 2001. We will never know whether such a convenient connection between that surah and the date are related, but it makes for a pretty convincing polemic.

is expected, it's not as effective. Perhaps that is why nothing happened.

What I am more interested in, however, is how the stories that ran for at least twenty-four hours about an impending terrorist attack on US soil adversely impacted our willingness to engage in conversations and relationships with Muslims in our communities, not only on that day, but on all future days as well. I fear these stories rarely accomplish anything other than to increase our general suspicion of Muslims. If we are asked to report suspicious behavior, as the governor of New York encouraged people attending Fourth of July celebrations that year to do, we begin to see and expect suspicious behavior by Muslims we encounter.

This isn't an argument against trying to be safe. What I am arguing is that our concern for safety can actually increase our lack of safety. When we allow the fear narrative to take root in our subconscious, we inevitably build up walls that are ever more difficult to break down between *us* and *them*. When we allow our fear to keep us separate from people who believe differently than we do or who look different, we begin to think that *they* are all out to get us, and our world continues to be unsafe.

The greatest action we can take in our communities to make them safer is to love our neighbors as we love ourselves and do the same with strangers and enemies. When we choose to engage in relationships with people, to become friends with the *other*, we no longer have much to fear.

The best defense against our collective fear of the other is to get to know and seek to understand them. It seems obvious, but it is far from it. The more we allow strangers to be strange to us, the more our fears will increase and the more we will choose to keep our distance from them.

This is why I refuse to listen to the voices in our culture that tell me to be afraid of strangers or refugees or Muslims. Instead, I'm learning to find ways to engage in relationships with people across lines of difference in order to make myself more loving and safe and to make my community a more loving, safe, and peaceful place. The way we see strangers, as well as the way we treat strangers, bears a lot of weight on how safe our communities are. When a society sends a message to immigrant populations, like refugees from Syria for instance, that they are not welcome, our safety *is* threatened. We have the choice to either make neighbors or enemies out of strangers. May we learn to make the former our reality.

4
Enemies (Part 1)

But I say to you that listen, Love your enemies, do good to those who hate
you, bless those who curse you, pray for those who abuse you...But love
your enemies, do good, and lend, expecting nothing in return. Your reward
will be great, and you will be children of the Most High; for he is kind to
the ungrateful and the wicked. Be merciful, just as your Father is merciful.

- Luke 6:27–28, 35–36 (NRSV).

We Can't Live without Them

I hate motorcycles. More specifically, I hate the sound of motorcycles. It is an abrasive and annoying mode of transportation. I hate motorcycles in my neighborhood and motorcycles on the freeway (especially in traffic). I hate motorcycles at stoplights and motorcycles in parking lots. I hate how motorcyclists want me to see them, but when I am on my bicycle, they don't seem to see me. Before you think that was a random thought, just the other day, I was heading out for a short (twenty-mile) ride on my road bike, when a motorcyclist pulled out directly in front of me. For some reason, despite my bright-orange cycling jersey (featuring the Grinch), my bright-yellow helmet, and my bike with bright-red handlebar tape, this motorcyclist did not or chose not to see me. As the irony of the situation hit me, I yelled, "Start seeing bicyclists!" as he nearly made *me* put on *my* brakes. He couldn't hear me, of course, because his motorcycle was so loud. I grumbled about this for at least five miles of my ride, to myself (and now to you).

My disdain for motorcycles, particularly the loud ones, causes me to hate the riders of the loud motorcycles. Now, not only are loud motorcycles the bane of my existence, but all those who ride said loud motorcycles are now my enemies. I would rather they didn't exist.

At all.

If I never saw another motorcycle in my life, I would not only be happier, but I would also have fewer enemies in this world.[73]

I'm sure the same could be said by others about cyclists on their fancy road bikes who wear spandex and think that they belong on the road. It wouldn't surprise me to hear someone complain about me in the same way I complain about people on motorcycles. In many ways, I feel like I am treated like an enemy of American driver culture every time I ride my bike on a two-lane country road. On another occasion, a garbage man yelled, "Get off the road!" out of his window at me as he passed me by while I was cycling (I seriously can't make this stuff up). I'm sure, with the shoe on the other foot, he would say he would be happier and would have fewer enemies in this world if cyclists ceased existing.

We all do this, don't we? Like I have said before, we have an incomparable ability to make enemies of anyone and everyone we don't like, don't understand, or fear. Enemy making is profoundly easy these days. The American media machine is incredibly adept at helping us find new enemies that we didn't even know existed. But, now that we do, we wish they didn't exist at all. Facebook is good at this too. A while back, one of my *friends* on Facebook wrote something completely absurd on his wall; he would donate ten dollars to Planned Parenthood every time one of his *friends* writes something about the media ignoring abortions in favor of Cecil the

---

[73] Unfortunately, this isn't hyperbole. To all of my friends and readers who love motorcycles, I don't understand you. Maybe it's time I sat down with a motorcyclist to find out what the fascination is with these loud machines. It probably *is* time for that.

lion, who became famous solely for being shot by a dentist for sport. Although the logic of this statement was lost on me, what I do know is this: anyone who disagreed with him was no longer his friend. The line had been drawn in the proverbial sand, and we were left to choose sides.

It's one thing when we make enemies out of motorcyclists or antiabortionists, whether in jest or in reality. It's another thing entirely when we make enemies out of entire people groups, whether on the basis of religion, race, or tribe. A cursory look through history tells a grim tale of violence and evil done between enemies of religion, race, and tribe. We know of the Crusades, of the Tutsis and Hutus, the Nazis and the Jews, the Israelis and the Palestinians, the Russians and the Americans, and the North and the South in the Civil War. Each conflict continues to have lasting effects on the collective subconscious of the groups involved, often with far-reaching consequences. A German can't simply ignore what happened during World War II, and neither can a Jew. The Civil War has created permanent stereotypes in the North of the South and in the South of the North.[74] We still experience the lingering aftereffects of the Cold War whenever Russia makes a geopolitical maneuver. And the Crusades have left an imprint on Christian-Muslim relations despite having ceased almost eight hundred years ago.

It seems we can't get around history. We are doomed to always

---

[74] The Civil War is affectionately called "The War of Northern Aggression" in the South.

have enemies of one sort or another. Even Switzerland has enemies.[75] Because this is our reality, what are we to do with our enemies? Are we to say, "[There] can be no...parley with the enemy, no trusting conversation, because the enemy simply wants to convert you, kill you, or make you submit"?[76] Are we to wish or pray for their destruction? Are we to treat them with permanent suspicion or hostility? Are we to avoid them or at least not associate with them? And what if we can't avoid our enemies? What if our enemies are our literal neighbors or coworkers? Should we do whatever it takes to make their lives miserable in order to force them to leave the neighborhood or the company? On the flip side,

> What do I communicate to a man about the love of God by being willing to consider him an enemy? What do I say about personal responsibility when I agree to consider him an enemy when it is only the hazard of birth that causes us to live under different flags? How is it reconcilable with the gospel—good news—for the last word in my estimate of any man to be that, in a case of extreme conflict, it could be my duty to sacrifice his life for the sake of my nation, my security, or the political order which I prefer?[77]

If you have stayed with me this far, you likely can see where this is headed, but let me say it concretely. If we hope for peace, we need a different way of being in the world when it comes to how we interact

---

[75] Contrary to popular belief, Switzerland has, at least throughout history, had its fair share of enemies.
[76] Camp, *Who Is My Enemy?*, 4.
[77] John Howard Yoder, *The Original Revolution: Essays on Christian Pacifism* (Scottdale: Herald Press, 1971), 41.

with and treat our enemies. This is one area of life in which we cannot afford to allow the status to remain quo.

Setting the Framework

Instead of following the formula I have set forth in the previous two chapters, I have chosen to begin this discussion by focusing solely on the words of Jesus. There are two main reasons for this. First, Jesus's words are straightforward and counterintuitive and therefore set the framework for the discussion as it unfolds. Second, as a Christian myself, I think that these words of Jesus cut straight to the heart of the matter more than the Old Testament (or Jewish tradition) or Qur'an (or Islamic tradition). Therefore Jesus's words will be the starting point rather than the conclusion to this discussion. I believe once we grapple with the command Jesus gave to love our enemies, we will be better equipped to engage with the ways in which the other Abrahamic faiths have dealt with and continue to deal with their enemies.

There have been many arguments and conversations as a result of Jesus's command, "Love your enemies," found in Luke 6 and Matthew 5. Pacifists believe that these are the most concrete and indisputable words that Jesus ever said, followed closely by turning the other cheek and the ethic of nonviolence. Christians who are convinced that these words from Jesus are ridiculous and not meant for all people or all conflicts have gone to great lengths to prove that Jesus couldn't have meant what he said. Before we get into what it looks like to practically love our enemies, we need to look at what we can't rightfully say about this groundbreaking and culture-shifting way of being in the world that Jesus calls us to enact.

First, we can't say that loving our enemies is the primary or only message that Jesus taught. This popular statement by Jesus only shows up in two places in the Gospels, and it only takes the form of three words. No other New Testament author directly quotes these words of Jesus, as this was only a small portion of the message that Jesus sought to teach.[78] As we have already seen, Jesus taught and exemplified that we are to love all people, not simply our enemies. Second, we can't say that Jesus offered this command as a guaranteed way to convert our enemy into a friend. On the contrary, Jesus promised in all four Gospels that there will always be people in our lives who seek to make our attempts to follow his way miserable and next to impossible.[79] I am not making the point that loving our enemies is not the way that Jesus called us to live. It certainly is. I am simply acknowledging that there is much more to the message of Jesus than this command itself and that this command does not necessarily mean that we will succeed in making neighbors of our enemies by following it.

---

[78] John P. Meier's four-volume work on the historical Jesus argues convincingly that Christians often make too much of these words of Jesus, despite their uniqueness in philosophical and religious history. He is startled by this command, and rightfully so. I would argue that Christians often make too little of these words and aren't sufficiently startled by them, however.

[79] Matthew 5:11, 10:22; Mark 13:11–13; Luke 6:22–23; John 15:18–25, 16:1–33 (NRSV).

Love Your Enemy Instead

Jesus opened this conversation in Matthew 5 by saying, "You have heard that it was said, 'You shall love your neighbor and hate your enemy.' But I say to you, Love your enemies and pray for those that persecute you."[80] Nowhere in the Torah or the Old Testament is there a direct statement about hating one's enemy, let alone a command to hate one's enemy. So, what was Jesus referring to here? There is good evidence that Jesus may have been referencing the growing popularity of the teachings of the Essenes (those Jews who separated themselves from broader culture in order to practice a perfected version of Judaism) found in the Dead Sea Scrolls. Since Jesus's cousin and mentor, John the Baptist, was likely a member of the Essenes[81] and some of his disciples were following Jesus at the time of this statement, it makes sense to draw this conclusion based on the context of the passage.

The *Rule of the Community* was a Qumran document that was likely composed by the Essenes. This document was a part of the Dead Sea Scrolls which were discovered in the early twentieth century near the Dead Sea. In it we find a requirement made of those who want to be a part of the Essene community. They were "'to love all the sons of light'—that is, all the fellow members of the conventicle—and 'to hate all the sons of darkness'—all other human

---

[80] Matthew 5:43–44 (NRSV).
[81] This is a contested historical fact. To hear another perspective, see Reza Aslan's book *Zealot*.

beings, Jews and Gentiles alike (1QS 1:9–10)."[82] So, when Jesus said, "You have heard it said," he may simply have been referencing a growing attitude among at least the Essenes—if not a broader subsection of Jews—that they are to hate all nonpracticing and imperfect Jews, as well as all Gentiles. Since Jesus was a rabbi himself, he was following the pattern of the rabbis who came before him. He took a teaching that the people were familiar with and turned it on its head in order to explain the heart of God. In the way he expounded upon this command, Jesus turned our understanding on its head in a profound way.

The rationale that Jesus gave for why his followers should love their enemies is this: "For [God] makes his sun rise on the evil and the good, and sends the rain on the righteous and the unrighteous."[83] Since Jesus's goal was to show humanity what God is like and to call all people into the emulation of the Creator, he gave this command in order to remind us that God is the lover and sustainer of all human beings, good and evil alike. "The transforming initiative is to participate in the kind of love that God gives regularly: as God gives sunshine and rain to enemies as well as friends, so are we to give love and prayers to our enemies as well as our friends. It could hardly be clearer that the transformative initiative is participation in God's active presence and God's grace."[84] In essence, Jesus was

---

[82] Meier, *A Marginal Jew*, 537.
[83] Matthew 5:45 (NRSV).
[84] Glen H. Stassen and David P. Gushee, *Kingdom Ethics: Following Jesus in Contemporary Context* (Downers Grove: IVP Academic, 2003), 140.

telling us that we are to love our enemies because *that's what God does*. Being created in the image of God, we are to love all people as fellow image-bearers.

Be Perfect?

Despite the fact that this *seems* so clear, many arguments have been leveled to say that this is an impossible standard for most humans to attain, based on the conclusion to the passage: "Be perfect, therefore, as your heavenly Father is perfect."[85] The argument goes that since this statement about being perfect followed Jesus's command to love our enemies and since we cannot live up to that moral standard, we cannot be expected to love our enemies. If true, Jesus's call to perfection undercuts all of what he taught that we observed in the previous chapter and perhaps throughout his whole lifetime.

Much of this argument is the result of a shift in thinking that happened around the rise of Christendom—when Constantine and subsequent emperors made Christianity the religion of the Roman Empire. Prior to the rise of the Christian Roman Empire, Christians were a persecuted minority. These early Christians were faced with the choice to live a hate-filled life or to choose to transcend the pattern of the empire through love and peaceful, nonviolent resistance. After Constantine, "the sermon, with its teaching on love of enemies or doing good to those who do bad to you, was thought to

---

[85] Matthew 5:48 (NRSV).

pertain merely to the realm of the spiritual or the personal, not to the realm of the secular or politics."[86] Loving one's enemies is indeed a difficult political policy to hold when trying to expand or even protect an empire. A world power that operated on the policy of loving its enemies would not be a world power for long. So, instead of taking Jesus's command seriously in all facets of life, they saw this command to be limited to the realm of interpersonal relationships only. For instance, one might be able to love an enemy who is an oppositional coworker or conniving next-door neighbor, but America cannot be expected to act lovingly toward Iran. That would be truly impossible.

This logic is based upon a utilitarian ethic proposed by Thomas Aquinas. For Aquinas, there was a logical order to love. "We owe certain people more love than we do others, and we owe God the most love of all. That is not to deny that Christians ought to love everyone equally, but the 'equally' here means that 'all men ought to be loved equally insofar as we ought to wish for all of them the same good, viz., eternal life' (*On Charity Q.8, reply to obj.8*)."[87] What Aquinas was essentially saying is that the "good" or "love" that is to be given to all is not equal to the good or the love that is given to our closest friends, family, and neighbors—or fellow Christians. The love of enemy, for Aquinas, is simply to pray for their salvation/conversion to Christianity. When colonialism and the first

---

[86] Lee Camp, *Who Is My Enemy?*, 30.
[87] Darrell Cole, *When God Says War Is Right: The Christian Perspective on When and How to Fight* (Colorado Springs: Waterbrook Press, 2002), 64.

missionary efforts began, loving our enemies often meant working toward converting them. If they became Christians, then they were no longer our enemies. On the contrary, if violence is deemed necessary against our national enemy in order to preserve justice, then that violence is the most loving action we can take toward our enemy. We loved the life out of Osama bin Laden, at least according to this line of reasoning.

But this way of thinking misses the point of Jesus's words entirely and misunderstands what is meant by the word *perfect*. "[The] word here means *complete* or *all-inclusive*, in the sense of love that includes even enemies. This is the point that Jesus has been emphasizing in this teaching: the love of God's grace that includes the complete circle of humankind, with enemies in it as well, by contrast with tax collectors and Gentiles, who love only their friends."[88] This point is made even more explicit when we consider the conclusion statement that Jesus made in Luke 6, the other place in which Jesus called his followers to love their enemies: "Be merciful, just as your Father is merciful."[89] Jesus isn't calling us into a moral perfection (which is indeed impossible), but into a way of being in the world that works for the good of others through practical and tangible acts of compassion and service, even toward our enemies. Glen Stassen and David Gushee propose this as an alternate reading or perhaps a better translation of the verse in question: "'Be

---

[88] Stassen and Gushee, *Kingdom Ethics*, 141.
[89] Luke 6:36 (NRSV).

complete or all-inclusive, therefore, as your heavenly Father is complete or all-inclusive,' or perhaps, 'completely all-embracing, as your heavenly Father is completely all-embracing.'"[90] Indeed, this is the heart of all three commands being explored in this book—loving neighbors, strangers, and enemies. All of our religious narratives point us to this way of being toward others, in one way or another, because this is what we believe God is also like.

That's Nice, But...

It's all well and good to understand what Jesus was talking about when he told us to love our enemies, but is it actually something that anyone has tried? Has anyone heard the words the Jesus taught and put these words into action? Michael Hart, who wrote a book called *The 100*, about the one hundred most influential people in history, didn't think so. He placed Jesus third on his list, after the Prophet Muhammad and Sir Isaac Newton. Here is why.

> Now these ideas [about loving one's enemies]—which were not a part of the Judaism of Jesus' day, nor of most other religions—are surely among the most remarkable and original ethical ideas ever presented. If they were widely followed, I would have had no hesitation in placing Jesus first in this book. But the truth is that they are not widely followed. In fact, they are not even generally accepted. Most Christians consider the injunction to "Love your enemy" as—at most—an ideal which might be realized in some perfect world, but one which is not a reasonable guide to conduct in the actual world we live in. We

---

[90] Stassen and Gushee, *Kingdom Ethics*, 341.

do not normally practice it, do not expect others to practice it, and do not teach our children to practice it. Jesus' most distinctive teaching, therefore, remains an intriguing but basically untried suggestion.[91]

These are difficult words. It seems that in our collective apathy, or perhaps our general acceptance that we will always have enemies, we have not done much to take Jesus's words as they are and to put them into practice when it comes to loving our enemies.

It is true what Hart claims when he says that these words of Jesus were not a part of the Judaism of Jesus's day nor were they a part of most other religious systems. Indeed, looking at the Torah, the Wisdom literature, the writings of the Qumran community (mentioned earlier), and ancient philosophers, such as Seneca and Aristeas, John P. Meier concludes that there is no iteration as short and as to the point as the simple (but not simplistic) command "Love your enemies."[92] That is not to say there aren't hints of similar ideas in these writings, however. The difference between Jesus's command and all of the others is that the command of Jesus is not the least bit self-interested. Unlike the commands in the Jewish Scriptures, Jesus doesn't say this with a rationale that says, "Do this because God will reward you." Rather, we are to do this because of the simple fact that this is the way God is. That may be why we don't have many examples in history of people actually putting his words into

---

[91] Michael Hart, *The 100: A Ranking of the Most Influential Persons in History* (New York: Citadel, 1978), 20–21.
[92] John P. Meier, *A Marginal Jew*, 531.

practice.

One might object by bringing up Dr. Martin Luther King Jr. or Gandhi and how these people took Jesus seriously and started revolutions in their respective countries. While this *may* be true, one could also say that King and Gandhi put Jesus's ethic of nonviolence into action more than his command to love their enemies. And, as Meier points out, "Nonviolence, nonretaliation, and love of enemies do not necessarily mean the same thing."[93] What he means is that it is entirely possible to choose to practice nonviolent resistance (such as turning the other cheek) without actually having love as the motivation for that resistance.

Love that Transforms (Potentially)

It is important to keep in mind that the love we are talking about is not a warm feeling toward another. We may not ever *feel* that way about our enemies. They are, after all, our enemies. What this love compels us to do is to *act* in a certain, practical, and tangible way toward all people that demonstrates compassion and works for their good, regardless of our relationship status. "He is…commanding his disciples to will good and to do good to their enemies, no matter how the disciples may feel about them, and *no matter whether the enemies remain enemies despite the goodness shown to them.*"[94] This brings up two equally opposite points, which

---

[93] Ibid., 529.
[94] John P. Meier, *A Marginal Jew*, 530.

lead to transformation.

First, if you are committed to acting compassionately and for the good of your enemy, it will inevitably lead to an actual transformation inside of *you*. No longer will you see your enemy as simply an enemy but as someone who deserves and receives your love. One practical way that we can love our enemies is to forgive them for the wrong they have done to us and for the wrongs we perceive to have been done to us. In fact, above all other practices, one could argue that forgiveness was Jesus's main focus when it comes to acting lovingly toward others. If God forgives us, how can we not forgive the enemy who has wronged us?

One night, after Christmas, our car was broken into in our driveway. We didn't make it difficult, since breaking into our car meant simply opening the door. We aren't door-lockers (which is probably not surprising). The reason this situation stood out in particular is that my wife had stashed the Christmas money she had received as well as our kids' Christmas money in the glove box, totaling about four hundred dollars. However crazy that might sound, that's what happened. Obviously, the money was stolen. Christmas is a big deal for my wife, and she *was* devastated not so much because *her* money was gone but because our kids' money was gone. That year, the Grinch truly stole Christmas.

Knowing that the culprits likely lived in our neighborhood, my wife decided to engage in a radical act of loving forgiveness. She bought a big fluorescent-green poster board and painted on it in big red letters, "To those who stole money out of our car, we forgive you." She then took it out to our front yard and nailed it on a tree facing the street. Now everyone on our street and everyone who drove by our house knew that we had been robbed and that we were choosing forgiveness rather than retaliation. That act of forgiveness transformed my wife's anger toward our anonymous enemies. She was able to move on without harboring hatred or fear or resentment in her heart.

Second, if you are committed to acting compassionately and for the good of your enemy, it will become very difficult for your enemy to continue to hate you. It is incredibly exhausting to hate someone who insists on loving you back. This is especially important when thinking about groups of people who commonly associate the *other* as their enemies, such as Palestinians and Israelis. Israeli Rabbi Arik Ascherman, who has become for me a modern-day saint, relates a story from his own life of how transformative love is not only for the one acting lovingly but also for the enemies who receive that love.

A settler was shooting at the feet of an older Palestinian man, and I stepped between them. When the army finally arrived and began to separate Israelis from Palestinians, I looked like one more settler with my beard and kippah, and they wanted me to move to where the settlers were standing. However, I pointed to the Palestinians and said, "I'm with them." This was simply a statement of fact on my part. However, one of the

Palestinians who was present reminded me of this later...The statement "I'm with them" had huge implications in his eyes. The truth is that, rather than being seen as "with the Israelis" or "with the Palestinians," I see myself as "with humans." What was intended as a simple statement of fact on my part was heard as an unusual declaration of our common humanity. There is an incredible need for solidarity, which can only happen when enemies become friends.[95]

It's hard for me to imagine how powerful that statement was to the Palestinians who had witnessed his act of justice on their behalf or for the Israeli officers to whom it was said. Ascherman isn't simply an Israeli Jew. As a rabbi, he is a representative of what it *means* to be an Israeli Jew. However small the action might have been, to the witnesses, it was profound—if a rabbi was *with* them, then perhaps there was hope that not all Jews were the enemy. When I read this story, I couldn't help but notice his words about being "with humans." His love caused him to identify with those whom his own people had oppressed. And that identification transformed his nation's enemies into his personal friends. Although this may not always happen, it is clear that when we choose to love our enemies, we greatly increase the potential of mutual transformation—from enemies into friends.

---

[95] Clark, *Abraham's Children*, 96–97.

Interlude

Tisha B'Av and Al-Aqsa

To get a good idea of why, for over sixty years now, peace has not come between the Palestinians and the Israelis, you only need to look to the Al-Aqsa mosque, located on the old Temple mount in Jerusalem. The Al-Aqsa mosque was originally built in Jerusalem in AD 705, and it has stood in its current iteration since AD 1033. Islamic tradition holds that the Prophet Muhammad was transported there in a dream, and as a result, Jerusalem was the direction of prayer for the Muslim community in Yathrib (Medina) prior to being changed to Mecca. The mosque wasn't built until about a hundred years after the death of Muhammad, but the Muslim people have always regarded Jerusalem to be a holy site, third only to Mecca and Medina.

The Al-Aqsa Mosque is built upon the very mount on which the second temple in Jerusalem was built prior to being destroyed by the Romans in AD 70. The western or Wailing Wall in Jerusalem, where Jews and some Christians go to pray regularly in Israel, is the western wall of the temple. Not surprisingly, a skirmish breaks out between Israeli Jews and Palestinian Arabs here on the day of Tisha B'Av (the ninth day of 'Av) almost every year.

Tisha B'Av is a Jewish holiday commemorating the destruction of the second temple in AD 70 and the first temple in 586 BCE, both of which occurred on the same day, the ninth day of the month of 'Av. On this day, many Jews fast in remembrance of these tragic events in the life of Israel and Judaism. It is no wonder that the Al-Aqsa mosque serves as a constant reminder that there still is no temple in Jerusalem. For Jews, no temple means that there is no sacrificial system or religious cult of worship within the life of the Jewish people. For almost two thousand years, no sacrifice has been made in Israel or anywhere else. That's kind of a big deal for Jews.

Does Tisha B'Av and the presence of the Al-Aqsa mosque mean that there will be and in fact can be no peace between Jews and Arabs, between Israelis and Palestinians, or between Muslims and Jews? Not necessarily.

Arik Ascherman, the Israeli Jewish rabbi I have mentioned already several times, wrote about his work for peace between Israel and Palestine in the book *Abraham's Children*. In it, Ascherman relates his work on Tisha B'Av to help rebuild the homes of Palestinians that have been destroyed by Israeli settlers in the West Bank. Here are some of his words regarding why he has made this part of his practice of faith.

> [Even] though Judaism rejects any depiction of God, we believe that there is an Image of God in this world. It is the human: "And yet there is something in the world that the Bible does regard as a symbol of God. It is not a temple or a tree, it is not a statue or a star. The symbol of God is man, every man" (quoting Abraham Joshua Heschel). So the ancient Midrash

124

teaches us that when we harm a fellow human, we are attacking God and diminishing God's Image in the world...

In 2005, twenty-two homes were demolished in the tiny village of Khirbat Tana and only one home was left standing. I observed the Tisha B'Av fast on a hot summer day while helping to rebuild those homes. The Tisha B'Av fast commemorates the destruction of the two Jewish temples that once stood in Jerusalem...

[The] destruction of a home demolishes the family that was living in it. For that family, the demolition is every bit as much of a tragedy as the tragedy we mourn on Tisha B'Av...Part of the spiritual ability to see God's Image in others is to be able to make the emotional connection between their oppression and ours, without feeling that making the connection negates the unique aspects of our personal and collective experiences.[96]

For Ascherman, it seems the key is the understanding that all humans share the divine image, or the breath of Allah, and are therefore worthy of our love, concern, care, and acts of compassion and reconciliation. If an Israeli Jewish rabbi can see this, I have hope not only that peace is possible but that reconciliation is possible between Israelis and Palestinians, between Jews and Arabs, and between all Muslims and all Jews.

Tragedy is tragedy. We *should* mourn the destruction of the two temples in Jerusalem alongside our Jewish neighbors, for those moments fundamentally altered the practice of Judaism. We should also mourn the destruction of Palestinian homes by Israeli settlers in the West Bank, for those moments continue to fundamentally alter

---

[96] Clark, *Abraham's Children*, 87, 91–92.

the daily lives of those affected. For, as Ascherman pointed out, as bearers of the divine image, we have the ability to empathize with the oppression of Jews and Palestinians without diminishing the reality of both.

Taking Ascherman's example as we look to how Judaism and Islam have engaged in conversations around loving one's enemies, perhaps we will see that there is hope that through relationships we can find real and lasting peace—not despite our religious beliefs but because of them.

5
Enemies (Part 2)

If your enemies are hungry, give them bread to eat; and if they are thirsty, give them water to drink; for you will heap burning coals of fire on their heads, and the LORD will reward you.

- Proverbs 25:21–22 (NRSV).

Repay injury with conduct more becoming and, behold, the person with whom you are at enmity becomes like an intimate friend. - Qur'an 41:34, trans. by Tarif Khalidi

The New Taliban

"I left the Azov because it was full of pagans. Committed _____s in the Azov were not allowed to stop to pray throughout the day—I needed a unit of _____s, a closely knit unit of committed _____ warriors. When two or three _____s gather around, they have God with them, and victory is guaranteed to be with us."[97] So, how did you fill in those blanks? My first impulse when reading that quotation is to assume that a Muslim extremist spoke these words. We are so accustomed to seeing these types of statements from Muslim radicals that, likely, if you've been reading or paying attention to news from America or anywhere else in the world over the last fifteen years, you automatically inserted "Muslim" into the blanks as well. I wouldn't blame you.

The reality may be surprising to you, however. In Ukraine, a small but growing militia formed in 2015 that was determined to fight Russia forever, until "European traditions and the…mindset of the 13th century" were finally set in place.[98] Again, this sounds a lot like the good ol' Taliban that we associate with everything from oppression of women to terrorism and bin Laden. And you're right. It *does* sound like the Taliban.

---

[97] "'Christian Taliban's Crusade on Ukraine's Front Lines," *Al Jazeera* English, last modified April 15, 2015, accessed August 20, 2015, http://www.aljazeera.com/indepth/features/2015/04/taliban-crusade-ukraine-front-lines-150414125522623.html.

[98] *Al Jazeera* English, "'Christian Taliban's Crusade on Ukraine's Front Lines."

You're also wrong. This militia was made up of Christians. When I read this story, I thought about what it communicated to Muslims and Jews about Christianity. The headline, "'Christian Taliban's Crusade on Ukraine's Front Lines," was inflammatory. It was not inflammatory because it was stretching the truth, but because it used the words *Christian*, *Taliban*, and *Crusade* in the same sentence. I, for one, did not want my Muslim and Jewish friends, cousins, and neighbors to read that headline and conclude that Christians were starting the Crusades again. The Crusades were a very dark period for Christianity as a world power, as well as a dark period for Muslims and Jews. I also wanted my Christian brothers and sisters to recognize that *we are not immune to radicalism related to our religion*. As Pope Francis remarked in his speech to the US Congress in the fall of 2015,

> Our world is increasingly a place of violent conflict, hatred and brutal atrocities, committed even in the name of God and of religion. We know that no religion is immune from forms of individual delusion or ideological extremism. This means that we must be especially attentive to every type of fundamentalism, whether religious or of any other kind.[99]

It serves no one for us to deny that these guys in the Ukraine are Christians because they like the way the Taliban went about practicing their faith in God.

---

[99] "Transcript: Read the Speech Pope Francis Gave to Congress," *Time*, last modified on September 24, 2015, accessed on September 27, 2015, http://time.com/4048176/pope-francis-us-visit-congress-transcript.

This story, this fundamental truth, is helpful for us as we frame our discussion moving forward. In the previous chapter, I went in depth in explaining what Jesus meant when he told us to love our enemies. The reality, however, is that most Christians are very willing to ignore Jesus (something that we touched on briefly as well). Before we look at how Islam and Judaism view the treatment of enemies, it is helpful for us to pause and remember, humbly, that Christianity has just as poor of a track record when it comes to loving our enemies, in the past as well as today. Christians all over America, in response to the terrorist attacks in Paris, loudly objected to allowing refugees from Syria to immigrate to the United States. Jesus's words may be the guide to turning our enemies into neighbors, but we are in many ways far from making that a reality.

One Sura, Two Sura, Three Sura, Four

The opening chapter of the Qur'an, also known as the *bismallah*, is prayed by Muslims up to seventeen times per day. At each of the five prayer times, it is recited three times, and devout Muslims will pray it two more times for various reasons. It is a good starting place for anyone who wants to get a feel for what drives the faithful practice of Islam for Muslims. These words are literally on the lips of Muslims from before the sun rises to after the sun sets every single day.

Praise be to God, Lord of the Worlds;

Merciful to all,

Compassionate to each!

Lord of the Day of Judgment.

It is You we worship, and upon You we call for help.

Guide us to the straight path,

The path of those upon whom Your grace abounds,

Not those upon whom anger falls,

Nor those who are lost.[100]

With these words, Muslims ask God to show them the way that leads to life, the straight path. It serves as a centering prayer for daily living, much like the Christ prayer in Christianity or the Shema in Judaism.[101]

The bismallah, which is beautiful and clearly benign, has also been a source of anti-Jewish and anti-Christian sentiment in Islam. How so? Ibn Kathir, a trusted and renowned interpreter/translator of the Qur'an from the fourteenth century, associated the final two lines of the prayer with Jews and Christians.[102] For Kathir, the Jews are the ones upon whom anger falls and the Christians are those who are lost. While no one may know how Kathir came to his conclusion, given that the Arabic gives no indication that this is a correct or

---

[100] Qur'an 1.

[101] The Christ prayer is a simple monastic prayer, often accompanied by the use of prayer beads. "Lord Jesus Christ, Son of God, have mercy on me, a sinner." The Shema, which is also the statement of faith in Judaism, is this: "Hear, O Israel, the Lord is God, the Lord is One. You shall love the Lord your God with all your heart, with all your soul, and with all your might."

[102] Tarek Fatah, *The Jew Is Not My Enemy: Unveiling the Myths that Fuel Muslim Anti-Semitism* (Toronto, McLelland and Stewart Ltd., 2010), 87.

faithful translation, his commentary on the bismallah has shaped much of how Muslims understand the meaning of the prayer to this day. This is another prime example of how interpretation can add meaning to a text. Without Ibn Kathir, this prayer is simply a prayer for guidance. With his interpretation, it is also a prayer that asks God to keep Muslims from following the paths of the Jews and the Christians. Even though this is likely not the purpose of the bismallah as it was originally revealed to the Prophet Muhammad, thanks to interpretation, it has become more than it was intended to be.

Obviously, this is problematic when it comes to Muslim-Jewish-Christian relations. If many Muslims are praying the bismallah seventeen times a day, and in their minds, they are praying against the *kuffar* (or enemies of Islam—including Jews and Christians), it is easy to assume that it becomes a steel reinforcement of animosity against over 2.5 billion people. It also reinforces an idea that God is on the side of Muslims and against everyone else. Not all Muslims see the bismallah in this way. There are Qur'an scholars who do not support Ibn Kathir's interpretation of this text. However, the fact that scholars disagree does not change how the common person has understood the meaning of the Qur'an throughout the past seven centuries. Can we acknowledge at this point that the greatest opponent to peace and friendship between us may be the authorities on revealed scripture who are charged with making meaning of the scriptures?

"You will surely find that the most hostile of men to the believers are the Jews and those who ascribe partners to God."[103] Islamic extremists have held up this verse as a clear indication that God is against the Jews and perhaps most Christians, as they ascribe to the doctrine of the Trinity. Logic follows that Muslims should also stand against them. One can see how this verse and Ibn Kathir's interpretation of the bismallah work hand in hand. In fact, citing this verse, Egyptian cleric Muhammad Hussein Yaqub said on national television in Cairo in 2009, "The Jews are our enemies. Allah will annihilate them at our hands. This is something we know for certain. We know this for certain—not because I say so, but because Allah said so. You shall find that the people strongest in enmity to the believers are the Jews and the polytheists."[104] It's pretty hard to argue with that interpretation. It certainly seems that this verse is very straightforward.

But, as we all know, nothing is straightforward when it comes to the interpretation of scripture. Yaqub is guilty of something that scholars refer to as *eisegesis,* or reading meaning into a text from outside the text. We do this all the time when we want to lend weight to our own arguments from scripture. For instance, a Christian might say that since Jesus told his disciples to gather swords in Luke 22:36, that means that Jesus should not be understood to be nonviolent or pacifistic. People who make that argument believe that violence *does*

---

solve some of the world's problems, and because of that belief, they read that meaning into the text, without paying attention to the context of the verse. It serves to justify the reader's position. However, when Jesus was later confronted by the arresting mob in the garden and Peter drew his sword and cut off the ear of a soldier, Jesus rebuked him ("No more of this!") and healed the soldier's ear.[105] In Matthew's version of the story, Jesus said to Peter, "Put your sword back into its place; for all who take the sword will perish by the sword."[106] While we might have to struggle to understand *why* Jesus told his disciples to gather swords, we certainly can't simply make the argument from one verse that Jesus loves violence. The context doesn't support the argument, both the immediate context of the verse in question as well as the entire context of Jesus's life and ministry.

The same goes for Yaqub. Immediately following Qur'an 5:82, we read this: "And you will surely find that the nearest in amity towards the believers are those who say: 'We are Christians,' and that is because among them are priests and monks, and they do not grow proud."[107] Of course, you might argue that Yaqub was declaring that Jews are the enemies of Islam, not Christians. This is true. Yaqub certainly focused his attention on the Jews. But Christians are definitely not out of mind in the verse above, as we have seen. If we look earlier in the same chapter, however, we see this: "Say: 'O

---

[105] Luke 22:51.
[106] Matthew 26:52.
[107] Qur'an 5:82–83.

People of the Book, you follow no religion unless you practice the Torah and the Gospel and what has been revealed to you from your Lord'...But those who believe, *as well as the Jews*, Sabeans and Christians who believe in God and the Last Day and do righteous deeds—no fear shall fall upon them, nor shall they grieve."[108] Regardless of what meaning one wants to make of Qur'an 5:82 and its statement against the Jews, it has to be reconciled with what we find in the whole context of the revealed scripture. In this case, it is at least difficult if not impossible to make the argument that the Jews (or the Christians) are simply and conclusively the enemies of God and therefore the enemies of Islam, at least with a straight face.

It is not my intention here to wrangle about scripture in order to prove that Muslims, Christians, and Jews are *not* enemies. We are, and have been, enemies. Regardless of how our scriptures are interpreted, history demonstrates that we have been enemies that have carried out much violence upon each other. However, my intention *is* to show that much of the argument that is made on the basis of Qur'anic Scripture for these actions is questionable if not unwarranted.[109] Before moving away from the Qur'an, let us take a look at one verse that can give guidance to Muslims on how God expects them to treat their enemies according their scriptures.

---

[108] Qur'an 5:67–68, italics added.
[109] For a good read on how the Hadith, or traditional sayings of Muhammad, have influenced Muslim-Jewish relations throughout the centuries, look at Tarek Fatah's *The Jew Is Not My Enemy.*

Intimate Friends

When I asked my friends Jamal and Hussein to help me understand how Islam deals with the concept of loving one's enemies, they were quick to point out that nowhere does the Qur'an or Islam teach or command a Muslim to love his or her enemies. In fact, both of them acknowledged that Muslims are commanded to deal harshly with their enemies, especially when religion is the basis for the fight. Hussein went so far as to say that the very concept of commanding someone to love is ridiculous to him. How could God command a person to feel a certain way toward another? However, despite that sentiment, they both pointed me to the following verse: "Repay injury with conduct more becoming and, behold, the person with whom you are at enmity becomes like an intimate friend."[110]

There is that word *enmity* again. If you recall, that's the word Yaqub used when declaring his jihad on the Jewish people, based on Qur'an 5:82. If enmity doesn't bear much meaning for you, I propose this as a helpful translation of the verse above: "Repay injury with conduct more becoming and, behold, the person who *you* are *actively opposing or feel hostility toward* or *who is actively opposing or hostile toward you* becomes like an intimate friend." This is key. Enmity is a two-way street of hostility and opposition. Red Sox fans and Yankees fans are at enmity with one another. Tom and Jerry are at enmity with one another. Liberals and Conservatives are at enmity

---

[110] Qur'an 41:34.

with one another. According to the Qur'an, Jews (and polytheists and Christians) and Muslims are at enmity with one another too. The word itself requires a healthy dose of the religious humility that Pope Francis was calling for. It's not just those guys over there who are hostile or opposing us. We are also hostile and opposing them as well. And this verse tells Muslims how they are to act toward their enemies (should we say enmities?). Treat them with kindness, and they will become like your friends.

The verse goes on to say that this isn't easy and doesn't often happen, but God is capable of making the seemingly impossible act of turning an enemy into a friend into a reality. How do we know? Well, that's because God sends rain on the dead, dry earth and brings it back to life. If he's capable of doing that, he is capable of transforming our most difficult and contentious relationships into friendships. With God, we could say, all things are possible. I would be guilty of eisegesis myself if I didn't acknowledge that, throughout the chapter in which this verse is found, there is assurance that the enemies of God will burn forever in hellfire.[111] I don't know what to do with that.

---

[111] Other verses that give me pause are these: "O believers, do not adopt My enemy and yours as comrades" and "O believers, do not ally yourselves with people on whom God's wrath has fallen" (60:1, 12). Interestingly, in the middle of this chapter, we find this verse: "Perhaps God will create affection between you and those among them with whom you were at enmity, for God is Omnipotent, and He is All-Forgiving, Compassionate to each" (60:6). If you want to understand what these verses mean, it would be best to ask your Muslim friend what he or she thinks.

What I do know, given what we have just considered, is that it is impossible to come to a conclusion about how the Qur'an commands Muslims to act toward their enemies without wrestling with the apparent contradictions in the text. And, as I have demonstrated, it is possible that there is at least a hint within Islam that through our actions of compassion and concrete goodness toward our enemies, those enemies can become like friends. Muslims are free to choose which narrative they wish to live by—that Jews and Christians are enemies or that Jews and Christians, though enemies, can become like intimate friends. We choose the lens through which we read our sacred texts, and that lens has ramifications for how we live in relation to all people.

Abraham's Children

Israel's history is filled with violence toward enemies, commands from God to annihilate enemies, and a general feeling of suspicion and avarice toward Gentiles. There is good reason why Israel has this sort of general opposition to or hatred of all enemies. From the four-hundred-year Egyptian slavery to the destruction of two temples by two Gentile nations, from their forced expulsion and execution in Spain in 1492 to the Holocaust, along with the ongoing conflict with their Arab/Muslim neighbors since the establishment of the nation of Israel in 1947, Israel has always been surviving threats from their enemies. With all of the suffering Jews have endured at the hands of oppressors, including Christians and Muslims, it is perhaps understandable that they aren't generally quick to jump at the notion of loving their enemies. Tolerate them? Sure. But love them? That could be dangerous.

However, a look at Scripture and midrash (teaching/interpretation by rabbis), as well as recent history, gives us a more balanced picture of how the Jewish people should live faithfully toward God in the way that they act toward their enemies. The story begins with Abraham and his two sons.

Abraham was an old man when he first heard from God. He also had a shorter name: Abram. He was wealthy, pagan, and childless. For reasons not given in scripture, God chose Abram to be his agent of blessing, through whom the entire world would be blessed. "I will make of you a great nation, and I will bless you, and make your name great, so that you will be a blessing. I will bless those who bless you, and the one who curses you I will curse; *and in you all the families of the earth shall be blessed.*"[112] Up to this point in the story, we have seen God shut Adam and Eve out of the garden for their disobedience (and for their protection); we have seen Cain kill his brother, Abel, and be cursed to walk the earth in isolation; we have seen a flood in which God destroyed almost all of humankind; and we have seen God scatter all people into different parts of the world with different languages. In the first eleven chapters of Genesis, we find a litany of acts and stories in which humankind was divided and isolated more and more from God and each other. But

---

[112] Genesis 12:2–3, italics added.

something changes with Abram. Now, in this man and his offspring, God has plotted goodness on all humankind for the rest of the story. Abram's mission in life is to be a blessing to everyone. As the story unfolds, that mission is extended to all Israel by fiat, being themselves children of Abraham.

For some, this is a familiar story. We remember the story of Abraham and Sarah; of the birth of the promised son, Isaac; of the attempted sacrifice of Isaac on an altar; and of the subsequent generations of descendants of Abraham and Isaac through exile in Egypt. But there is another son, the firstborn son of Abraham, who not only became a great nation but has also been vilified by both Jews and Christians throughout the centuries. That son is Ishmael, and Jews, Muslims, and Christians all agree that the Arab people descended from him.

The reason for the vilification of Ishmael and his descendants can be found in the scriptures themselves. Here are God's words concerning the future of Ishmael: "He shall be a wild ass of a man, with his hand against everyone, and everyone's hand against him; and he shall live at odds with all his kin."[113] Curiously, the Hebrew in this verse, which is often translated "at odds with," also means "to the east of." So, either God is saying that Ishmael will always be fighting with his stepbrothers (the Jews) or he will live to the east of them. Regardless, the text is clear. God tells Hagar, Ishmael's

---

[113] Genesis 16:12.

mother, that Ishmael's hand will always be against everyone else. This verse has been the explanation for why the Arabs/Muslims and the Jews have always and will always be fighting. Even in my Christian upbringing, this story was given as the reason for the lack of peace in the Middle East. It's as simple as the accident of birth. It's also a convenient narrative since it seems to be the case, at least in modern history.

Ishmael, meaning "God hears," was the name given to him by his mother, Hagar, when they were near death in the desert. Apparently, Abraham had a penchant for trying to kill his kids. Although I say this slightly tongue in cheek, it's also a part of the story. He sent Ishmael to the desert to die twice and even attempted to sacrifice his son Isaac on an altar. God heard the cries of Ishmael and Hagar, saved them from death in the desert, and promised to make him into a great nation. There's a midrash, Talmud Sotah, which tells a foundational myth that is vital to helping Jews understand how they are to treat the enemy.

> In one of the *midrashim* written by our sages so long ago, the angels come to God before God prepares the well and demand that God let Hagar and Ishmael die because of the future suffering the children of Ishmael will cause the children of Israel. God refuses their request and says, "Ba'asher hu sham" (right now in front of me is an innocent child). We, who are created in God's Image, are therefore commanded to be as God-like as humanly possible.[114]

---

[114] Clark, *Abraham's Children*, 92.

This takes us back to the very beginning of the story, in which we find that God creates humans in his image, both male and female. For Jews, this is a foundational belief; all humans are created in the image of God. Therefore, like God does in the midrash quoted above, as bearers of God's image, we are to treat even our enemies as fellow image-bearers. As we have seen over and over again, this is what God is like—bestowing his love on all people regardless of how they act toward God or others.

An important event happens later in the story of Isaac and Ishmael—the brothers who seem doomed to always live at odds with one another. When Abraham dies, Isaac and Ishmael come together to bury him. This is incredibly significant in tribal culture. If these two brothers really were enemies, as we are inclined to assume, they would not have reconciled their differences in order to do their duty as sons of Abraham. We would assume that Ishmael would not be present for this event, especially since the text also indicates that Abraham gave Isaac his blessing at his death. That blessing should have been given to Ishmael as the firstborn son, but instead it was given to Isaac. Even so, Isaac and Ishmael together buried their father.

Immediately following this event in the text, we see two lists: the descendants of Ishmael and the descendants of Isaac. We are told that Ishmael, like Isaac, had twelve sons and that each of these sons were princes of their tribes. These are their names: Nebaioth, Kedar, Adbeel, Mibsam, Mishma, Dumah, Massa, Hadad, Tema, Jetur,

Naphish, and Kedemah.[115] Any good Jew knows that names and descendants are important. These lists, which seem so mundane and tedious to many Christians, are the written history of a people in a place. They are attachments to the past, and sometimes, as in the case of Ishmael's descendants, they give us insight into the future.

In the book(s) of Isaiah, the prophet has a vision of the end of time, when all people will be gathered to the mountain of God and will seek to find truth there.

Arise, shine; for your light has come,

And the glory of the LORD has risen upon you

For darkness shall cover the earth,

And thick darkness the peoples;

But the LORD will arise upon you,

And his glory will appear over you.

Nations shall come to your light;

And kings to the brightness of your dawn.

Lift up your eyes and look around;

They all gather together, they come to you

Then you shall see and be radiant;

---

[115] Genesis 25:13–15.

Your heart shall thrill and rejoice,

Because the abundance of the sea shall be brought to you,

The wealth of the nations shall come to you

All the flocks of Kedar shall be gathered to you,

The rams of Nebaioth shall minister to you;

They shall be acceptable on my altar,

And I will glorify my glorious house...

Violence shall no more be heard in your land,

Devastation or destruction within your borders;

You shall call your walls Salvation,

And your gates Praise.[116]

Did you see it? The first and second sons of Ishmael are named here in Isaiah as accepted and invited to God's holy mountain at the end. This is not by accident either. The writer likely knows the list of Ishmael's descendants in Genesis 25 (he was a Jew after all), and he begins that list here as a literary device to remind the Jews of all of the descendants of Ishmael. As I have already mentioned, in an oral culture, these two names would conjure the entire list of descendants of Ishmael in the minds of the listener. Even if this isn't the case, the least we can say is that two of the twelve tribes of Ishmael are envisioned as participating in the coming kingdom of God that all Jews hope for in the end. So much for the narrative that says the sons

---

[116] Isaiah 60:1–4a, 5, 7, 18, italics added.

of Ishmael are forever the enemies of God and the Jews.

Even if my understanding of these scriptures is in error (which is entirely possible), these texts make it difficult to argue that because God says that Ishmael's hand will always be against his brothers, the Jews are free to treat them however they please. The Scripture and the midrash enjoin Jews to see Ishmael and his descendants as people created in the image of God for whom God has a special purpose on this earth and into the future. This vision of Isaiah illustrates that the Jews and Muslims (or at least Arabs) are not destined for perpetual enmity but for future worship together when God sets all things back to right.

Practicing Proverbs

In the portion of the Hebrew Scriptures referred to as "wisdom literature," we find a counterintuitive insight into the way God desires the Jewish people to treat their enemies. Proverbs 25:21–22 states, "If your enemies are hungry, give them bread to eat; and if they are thirsty, give them water to drink; for you will heap burning coals of fire on their heads, and the LORD will reward you." This is not simply a moral maxim, but a directive that falls in line with the Jewish concept of *tikkun olam*, or the healing of the world. Essentially, tikkun olam means that the primary task of the Jewish people on earth is to work on repairing the brokenness throughout creation—between human and God, human and creation, and human and human. If Jews are truly committed to tikkun olam, then this verse tells them one way in which they can participate in healing the brokenness of human relationships.

The proverb, which has traditionally been attributed to Solomon, includes a command as well as a rationale for the command, much like the commands of Jesus and Moses from the previous chapters. The command is simple: do good to those who wish to do you harm. Stated negatively, it could also be put as avoiding doing evil to those whom you consider to be your enemies. The rationale in this proverb is also straightforward: God will reward you for your actions and, you hope, reward your enemy by transforming that relationship.

There are many ways of understanding the idea of heaping burning coals of fire on the head of one's enemy. Some have considered this to be a sense of shame that may lead to repentance on the part of the enemy. Speaking on November 17, 1957, at the Dexter Avenue Baptist Church, Dr. Martin Luther King Jr. commented on the concept of transformation through good done toward one's enemies.

> [If] you hate your enemies, you have no way to redeem and to transform your enemies. But if you love your enemies, you will discover that at the very root of love is the power of redemption. You just keep loving people and keep loving them, even though they're mistreating you. Here's the person who is a neighbor, and this person is doing something wrong to you and all of that. Just keep being friendly to that person. Keep loving them. Don't do anything to embarrass them. Just

keep loving them, and they can't stand it too long. Oh, they react in many ways in the beginning. They react with bitterness because they're mad because you love them like that. They react with guilt feelings, and sometimes they'll hate you a little more at that transition period, but just keep loving them. And by the power of your love they will break down under the load.[117]

For some, this seems like simple speculation. There is no guarantee that any amount of loving action toward one's enemies will change the way one is treated by them. However speculative it may be, King's life bears witness to the fact that to "keep loving" is indeed a transformative act, especially in relation to the transformation of the hearts of the enemy. God willing, in our time, that transformation will come to full fruition.

One of Dr. King's companions, Rabbi Abraham Joshua Heschel, understood that the rationale for all of our actions for the good of our enemies is that even our enemies are created in the image of God.

My first task in every encounter is to comprehend the personhood of the human being I face, to sense the kinship of being human, solidarity of being...The human is a disclosure of the divine, and all men are one in God's care for man. Many things on earth are precious, some are holy, humanity is the holy of holies.[118]

---

[117] "Loving Your Enemies, Sermon Delivered at Dexter Avenue Baptist Church," *Martin Luther King Jr. and the Global Freedom Struggle*, accessed on September 24, 2015, http://kingencyclopedia.stanford.edu/encyclopedia/documentsentry/doc_loving_yo ur_enemies/.

[118] Abraham Joshua Heschel, "No Religion Is an Island," *Union Seminary*

We can never lose sight of the fact that our enemies also bear the divine image. When we do good unto them, we honor the image of God in them, and God will reward us accordingly for how we have treated them.

The Rehumanizing Effect of Lament

With God anything can be said. Without God nothing is heard. Without God what is said is not said.

—Elie Wiesel

Some of the most profoundly honest—and dark—passages in the Hebrew scriptures are found in what are called lament Psalms. These songs and prayers demonstrate the reality of human suffering and humanity's desire that God will deal with the evils of this world. "The task of lament is not simply to complain to God about injustice, but to *move God to be just*. These are prayers offered in the certain conviction that God must stay in the world as a God of justice."[119] If God *is* just or will act justly, then these Psalms are calling God to do what he says he will do in our time, here. They are a way of praying for what we know to be true to be realized in our time, even when we don't see it yet. So, within the Psalms of lament, we have this language that is raw and uncensored, especially toward enemies.

O God, do not keep silence;

Quarterly Review 21, no. 2, 1 (January 1966): 121.
[119] Samuel E. Balentine, *Prayer in the Hebrew Bible: The Drama of Divine-Human Dialogue*. (Minneapolis: Fortress Press, 1993), 286.

Do not hold your peace or be still, O God!

Even now your enemies are in tumult;

Those who hate you have raised their heads.

They lay crafty plans against your people;

They consult together against those you protect.

They say, "Come, let us wipe them out as a nation;

Let the name of Israel be remembered no more."

O my God, make them like whirling dust,

Like chaff before the wind.

As fire consumes the forest,

As the flame sets the mountains ablaze,

So pursue them with your tempest and terrify them with your hurricane.

Fill their faces with shame,

So that they may seek your name, O LORD.

Let them be put to shame and dismayed forever;

Let them perish in disgrace.[120]

At times, we all are faced with situations in which we are suffering. We feel anger about our situation and a desire to be delivered from that suffering. "This anger is not only spiritually liberated. It is psychologically honest."[121] These words give us permission to feel,

---

[120] Psalm 83:1–4, 13–17.
[121] Walter Brueggemann, *Praying the Psalms* (Eugene: Wipf and Stock Pub.,

to rage, and even to be open to the true desire within us that our enemies will be destroyed. The Psalms of lament not only give words to those feelings and desires, but they also remind us, and God, that it is not our fight.

This is why lament Psalms are so important to the conversation about how Jews are enjoined to treat their enemies. They are not prayers that ask God to give *us* strength to defeat our enemies. Rather, they are prayers that ask God to bring about the justice that he has promised to bring in regards to our enemies. "[The] complaint psalms are acts of hope. They articulate the deepest hurt, anger, and rage of Israel. But they are not statements of resignation, which accept the bad situation. Rather, they are insistences upon and expectations from God, who can and will, may and must, keep promises."[122] There is a certain therapeutic effect that these Psalms have on us. When we say what we truly feel, we are also participating in clearing the air of the darkness and despair that hovers over us in times of suffering. Voicing these desires for justice allows us to continue to act lovingly toward our enemies in full hope that someday God will do what he has promised.

For Jews, the fight against enemies is not their fight. It is God's fight. Indeed, if you were to read the accounts of the battles the Israelites fought against their enemies in the Hebrew scriptures, you

---

2007), 55.

[122] Brueggemann, *Praying the Psalms*, 58.

would see that the power to attain victory was always God's, not theirs. Jews are to act in ways that repair the world, to demonstrate their ability to acknowledge the divine image even in their enemies, and to work for peace with their enemies. God *will* vindicate all those who have been treated unjustly by others. That may very well be the reward of God on those who do good unto their enemies.

No Guarantees

For both Jews and Muslims, there is no guarantee that the enemy will be changed by one's goodwill toward them. The Qur'an states that God *may* do this, that he may choose to make an enemy into a friend for those who choose to repay evil with good. He also may not. Regardless, treating one's enemies with kindness demonstrates something about us. It demonstrates that we have hope that God will bring about justice, so we don't have to. It demonstrates that we are able to see the image of God, or the divine spark, even in our enemies. It demonstrates that we are unwilling to disrespect that divine image by taking vengeance into our own hands against our enemies. And it demonstrates that we have hope in God that someday things will be set to right, that peace will happen, and that we will be on the right side of God in the end.

Interlude

The Realest Problem and the Biggest Risk

My grandpa stated the obvious to me on the phone recently. He lives near Sun City, Arizona, where there are golf-cart crossing signs on almost every street—a true old-person's paradise. He has continued to serve the church since he turned twenty all the way to today, has written a book and a devotional study guide, and has a doctorate and an honorary doctorate from the Hindustan Bible Institute. He loves Jesus and deeply believes in what Jesus taught.

The obvious statement my grandpa said to me was this: "The people, specifically Muslims, whom you are trying to help people learn how to love, are the very people that most Americans are afraid of." He said something about all of the violence and turmoil going on right now in the world and said that pretty much everyone is afraid of Muslims. He gave one reason for why people are afraid of Muslims. We don't hear Muslims speaking out against the violence that Muslims are perpetrating in our world.

He wasn't saying this to me because he doesn't believe in what I do. He said this because he was reinforcing the importance of the work that I do. I told him that I have heard an imam tell Christians the exact same thing—that *he* doesn't hear Christians speaking out against the killing of innocent Muslims in the Muslim world through the use of military force and drone attacks. They are both right.

Christians aren't hearing Muslims, and Muslims aren't hearing Christians.

My friend Brian was on a radio show in Denver where a caller said the same thing my grandpa said to me about not hearing Muslims speaking out against Muslim violence. I think he and his friend Carl Medearis, who was also on the program, made a good point when they said that we aren't hearing the voices because we aren't listening for the voices. Instead of seeking out news sources that tell many sides of a story, we simply turn to CNN or Fox News, and neither is talking about Muslims who oppose terrorism.

And that's *part* of the problem.

The bigger problem is that we don't have any actual human relationships with people who are different from us and can tell us what they think about the things that really bother us. When we don't have relationships with people who are different from us, we won't believe news that tells us otherwise. The real problem is that we are afraid of what we don't know and what we don't understand. Even more, the realest problem is that we don't want to not be afraid and we don't want to know or understand what we are afraid of.

We don't want to love our neighbors.

We don't want to love strangers.

We don't want to love enemies.

As long as we keep the other at arm's length, we keep from humanizing them and we continue to fear and hate them. We make the other into an ideological entity instead of putting a face and a name on him or her. Ideologies are much easier to fear than human beings, aren't they?

But our only hope is to do whatever we can to develop friendships with people who are different from us. Our only hope is for Christians to stop othering Muslims and for Muslims to stop othering Christians. Our only hope is for Jews to stop othering Muslims, and for Muslims to stop othering Jews. Our only hope is for Jews to stop othering Christians, and for Christians to stop othering Jews. We other each other by only listening to what *our* people say about *those* people. We other each other by not engaging in meaningful conversations that lead to life-changing and life-giving relationships.

Life changing means that *we risk being changed* through the relationship.

Life giving means that we risk *letting our friend be changed* through the relationship.

We risk making friends out of enemies when we engage in dialogical friendships.

When we do this, we risk letting go of fear and putting on love. When we do this, we risk healing our communities, our culture, and our world. The question then is this: Are we willing to risk letting go of the fear that drives us to hatred and division in order to participate in healing the world here and now? Are we willing to engage in relationships with those who believe differently than we do in order to participate in the shalom that God is plotting and planning to bring to bear on our world?

6
Dialogical Friends

God's reconciliation of human beings, who were God's enemies, provides a
model for what it means for humans to reconcile. Thus to "achieve
religious peace" means to transform a relationship of possible enmity into
one of friendship. And to be a friend does not mean to deny differences but
rather to understand each other accurately, to treat each other with respect,
and to share with one another.[123]

—Martin Accad

---

[123] Volf, *A Common Word*, 65.

We Need a New Way

My wife and I were in the Imam's study after evening prayers. The walls were literally lined with gold-lettered books in Arabic. It was like stepping into a pastor's study at a church, only with entirely different content on the shelves. My goal was to find out from him what he felt would be beneficial for his community in terms of creating spaces for Muslims and Christians to get to know one another in our city. I have come to the slow realization, through reading books by James Cone and Cornell West, that as a white Christian man, my role is not one of dictating what I think would be the best for a minority group. Rather, my role is to listen and to do what I can to facilitate whatever said minority group thinks would be best for them and their community. With a ratio of about one to one hundred, Muslims are definitely a minority group in the United States. My wife's goal was to tell him about SE7EN FAST, an event we created in 2015 that encourages Christians to fast in solidarity with Muslims and to break fast with them as well on one day during Ramadan. As we sat there waiting, I was hoping that somehow Imam Salem would come up with the idea of Christians breaking fast with Muslims on his own so I didn't come across as an imperialistic white Christian.

Imam Salem and Yazan, the guy in charge of the youth group, walked in. We got reacquainted, which also involved Imam Salem making a remark about how my beard was trying to compete with his. To the contrary, my beard doesn't enter competitions, even with imams. As we talked, it became increasingly clear that this man was not pastoral but philosophical. A pastor is primarily concerned with the needs of the people in his or her care, while a philosopher is concerned with ideas and theories for why things are the way they are and making sure people think well. We need both types of leaders. At one point, he asked me what the benefit would be to the Muslim community to open their doors to Christians.

"Well, one benefit is that it creates an opportunity for friendships to be formed. And when a Christian has a Muslim friend, they have a human filter for the messages that we are given in the media. So, for instance, when a couple of Muslims shoot up a Prophet Muhammad cartoon-drawing contest, I can ask my friend if that is what Islam teaches. Likewise, he can ask me if I, as a Christian, believe that it's a good idea to hold such cartoon-drawing contests. Friendships help dispel fear, which will ultimately help us to learn to love each other better, right?"

Yazan smiled and nodded in agreement. Imam Salem wasn't as quick to agree. He explained that he was open to perhaps hosting a dialogue on a theological topic and letting people hear what Muslims and Christians think about various topics. In fact, he had done this at the church that neighbors the mosque, and the pastor of that church had done the same in the mosque. He told me that the pastor taught in their Sunday School for several weeks on the basic fundamentals of the Christian faith, leaving space for questions at the end. For him, as a philosopher, this was the best way to help his people know what

Christians believe and to learn to think critically about what they believe. The idea of simply hosting a night designed to let people meet one another and hear one another's stories was dangerous to him, because he could be opening his people up to Christians who would like to convert Muslims.

The problem with interfaith dialogues such as these is that information won't change human hearts, at least not very often.[124] Not many of us have had transformational moments, those moments in which we know we have been fundamentally changed, that involved simply hearing new information. More often, it's a combination of information and experience that leads to our transformation. As the axiom goes, I can know everything about climbing a fourteen-thousand-foot mountain. I can know what equipment is needed, how much water to drink, how much food to bring along, what risks are at stake, and even what the view from the top is like. But until I actually ascend a fourteener, I will never know the real majesty, nor will I have experienced the adrenaline-inducing drama of the top that causes people to do it over and over again. Knowledge goes hand in hand with experience. So, to simply host a *dialogue* between an imam and a pastor, though potentially valuable, will rarely be transformational for either community.

---

[124] Ironically, I am writing a book full of information with the intention of transforming the way people think about the "other."

Experiencing the Other

A few years ago, I was teaching a group of Christians in a rural community about Islam and how to build bridges with Muslims in our communities over the course of eight weeks. The model was this: a Christian teaches Christians about another religion and hopes to change their modus operandi toward that other religious community (i.e., information without experience). This particular rural community exists because of a desire for isolation. It is about twenty minutes from the city, and many of the people there have chosen to live in a white enclave outside of the city for reasons of safety and better educational opportunities for their kids. Many people call it the "white flight" destination, actually. This is one of the many mostly white communities in central Illinois surrounding the city of Peoria. One of the older ladies in the class had this explanation for why she was there.

"My son was in the Iraq war. All I know about Islam I have learned from him or from the news, and it's not good. I am afraid of Muslims. I'm here because I don't want to be afraid anymore."

Isn't that beautiful?

I was thankful that Ramadan was happening during this class and I was able to set up a night for our class to be able to break fast at the mosque with Muslims in the big city (with a different imam). The fearful lady participated, despite the fact that she had never met a Muslim, was afraid of Muslims, and was equally timid about simply being in the city. We met in the parking lot of the church I attended at the time, which was in one of the more diverse areas of the city. As we gathered together, I couldn't tell if the anxious looks on their faces were due to the urban surroundings or the fact that we were going to a mosque in a few minutes. I didn't help anything when I told the group, "I don't know what is going to happen when we go in there. All I know is that we will have to take our shoes off at the door." This was true-ish but not the whole truth. All I accomplished in saying this was to raise the level of anxiety felt by everyone from this monocultural rural community. I would be lying if I said I didn't slightly enjoy it.

When we entered, we indeed were invited to remove our shoes. Then the women were whisked away to the back part of the mosque—the women's area—while the men were taken to the front. A young, white convert to Islam named Eric (his Arabic name was Abd al-Haqq, meaning "Servant of Truth") welcomed us. He went on to share a bit about what Muslims believe and what they do to practice their faith. He told us about the five fundamental beliefs in Islam—the belief in one God, in angels and demons, in the holy books, the holy prophets, and judgment day. He shared about the five pillars as well, explaining that the pillars help Muslims demonstrate their beliefs in specific ways. Although unaware, Eric taught everything that I had been teaching this group of people for the previous seven weeks. It was a strange start to the evening in retrospect. Aside from about two minutes for mingling, we were invited to sit down and listen to an expert share some information with us, as if information transforms.

When Eric finished and the time for breaking fast was upon us, we all took a date and ate it. Eric explained that Muslims break fast by first eating a date because, according to Islamic tradition, that's what the Prophet Muhammad did. After this was the time for prayer. We watched as the whole gathered community of Muslims prayed together, with their bodies and their words. As we watched, I couldn't help but wonder what was going through the minds of the rest of the people in my group. This was not so strange to me, having lived in the Middle East and having taught at an Islamic school. But for white Christian people from rural America experiencing this for the first time, this had to have been fascinating. Not only was the entire gathered congregation praying in unison, but if Christians were fasting all day, they definitely wouldn't be praying for fifteen minutes before eating, at least not in my experience.

Finally the time came for breaking fast with a feast of epic proportions. There was food from Palestine, Pakistan, and Persia. Rice dishes, hummus, baba ghanoush, kafta, shawarma, stuffed grape leaves, and anything else you could imagine made up the spread of food. It was epic not only on account of the amount of food, which was impressive, but on account of the conversations, warmth, and hospitality that was offered to us. I kept hearing the women roaring in laughter in the back of the room. I had no idea what they might have been talking about, but whatever it was, they were connecting in a way that was mystical and true. Often the most mystical and beautiful moments of our lives happen across the table, don't they? How many times have you waited for the right moment to tell some big good news and that moment came in the intimacy of table fellowship? Eating together is a spiritual practice. And something profoundly spiritual was happening for those women.

The next evening, I had some time with this group to debrief their experience at the mosque the night before. The fearful lady who wanted to learn not to be afraid anymore said something incredibly significant to me. "Now I know that Muslims are people just like me." For city-dwellers, this statement seems to be pretty unremarkable. People in the city have a difficult time relating to the isolation and ethnocentrism of rural America. But, to me, having been raised in a rather large town of all white people, I understood her. This was the first time she had ever spent time with Muslims. Perhaps it was the first time she had really interacted with any sort of diversity, at least in a significantly long time. She was fundamentally changed by her experience across the table from those Muslim women. Instead of being afraid, she was able to see the humanity— and we could say the divine image—in them. And not only in them, but she was also able to see the divine image in all Muslims.

It's not enough just to hear information. We need experience. The way toward peace, toward making neighbors out of our strangers and enemies, is dialogical friendship.

Dialogical Friendship: Reciprocity

A dialogical friendship is a reciprocal relationship that is mutually life changing and life giving. Let me unpack that sentence a little further. A dialogical friendship gives and receives; that's what we call reciprocity or a reciprocal relationship. This is unnatural for most of us. We are used to monological relationships in which we give but we are often not open to receiving from the other. I am always willing to tell you what I believe, but I am less often willing to hear what you believe. That's why it's called monological; it consists of a monologue and being willing to talk to anyone who will listen. Monologues are part of the fabric of our divisions: I'll tell you what I believe. If you agree, then you're in. If you don't, then you're out. We do this with so many of our beliefs that it becomes hard to imagine another way of relating when it comes to the most important things. A dialogical friendship, on the contrary, follows this model: "Be quick to listen, slow to speak, and slow to become angry."[125] Rather than seeking first to be understood, the goal of a dialogical friendship is to understand the other.

"The question [is] how to have a vertical relationship with one's own understanding of the divine, and a horizontal relationship with the diversity of the world—in Cantwell Smith's words, to arrive at a point where one 'can appreciate other men's values without losing allegiance to our own.'"[126] So, reciprocal relationships require

---

[125] James 1:19 (NRSV).
[126] Eboo Patel, *Sacred Ground: Pluralism, Prejudice, and the Promise of America*

each person to be able to empathize with the other. Empathy is our way of getting into the shoes of other people to see things from their perspective or to seek to understand where they are and where they have come from. The key to empathy, however, is not *simply* the ability to get into the shoes of other people but also to sit with them where they are without trying to help them or change them. Empathy in relationships across lines of difference means fostering the ability to see the other person as equally convinced and equally faithful to his or her way of seeing or believing. This sort of reciprocal relational empathy requires us to be with the other person in his or her beliefs and experiences without necessarily questioning or challenging him or her. Brian McLaren has cleverly called this "with-ness."[127] Questions may come, but the first step is to simply understand. In a reciprocal relationship, each person must be open to what the other person has to offer, while still remaining committed to the belief that informs his or her faith.

In order to be mutually life changing and mutually life giving, the friendship needs to be based upon this idea of reciprocity. We are not only giving, but we are receiving. We are not only sharing the ideas and beliefs that we feel have revolutionized our way of seeing the world, but we are also hearing those unique beliefs of our friends. Looking back to my first conversation with Jamal, I see I was unabashedly sharing the ideas that had revolutionized my

---

(Boston: Beacon Press, 2012), 136.
[127] McLaren, *Why Did...?*, 237.

understanding of faith. As our relationship progressed, there was (and continues to be) a give-and-take to that conversation. A dialogical friendship will ultimately leave both friends fundamentally changed as a result and more capable of truly loving their own neighbors, strangers, and enemies.

Rabbi Abraham Joshua Heschel said that the fundamental prerequisite for interfaith relationships is faith.[128] In order to have something to offer in a dialogical relationship, each person has to come to the proverbial table with his or her own stories that inform his or her reason for believing. If we hope to understand one another, we have to first understand why it is we believe what we do, both about God and about humans. If we don't know what we believe, we don't have much to offer. If we are focused primarily on finding common ground, we give up so much of what makes us who we are in the process. "Moreover, at a time of paucity of faith, interfaith may become a substitute for faith, suppressing authenticity for the sake of compromise. In a world of conformity, religions can easily be leveled down to the lowest common denominator."[129] Dialogical friendships don't deny the uniqueness of belief. Rather, they push us to be able to articulate why we believe what we do. Dialogical friendships also require us to have a theological framework for why we think the relationship is important in the first place.

So, from a Christian perspective, I believe that God desires to

---

[128] Heschel, *No Religion Is an Island*, 125.
[129] Heschel, *No Religion Is an Island*, 126.

reconcile all human beings to himself because he has created each human being in his own image. God is not content to be estranged from his creation. In Jesus, God gave us the means to be reconciled to him, as well as the way to be reconciled with one another. I have been given a calling to love my neighbors as I love myself. I have been given a calling to love strangers as I love myself. And I have been given a calling to love my enemies in the same way that God does—unconditionally and without favoritism. I see this example played out in the life of Jesus, in his relationships with people from all sorts of religious backgrounds—the Samaritans, the Pharisees, the Gentiles, the Essenes, the Roman collaborators, and the terrorists. As the ultimate representation of what it means to be a human being, Jesus chose to love, to party, and to forgive impartially. As a Jew, Jesus brought his understanding of God and humans to each individual interaction. As I follow his example, I do the same.

Many Muslims I have interacted with share with me their belief that God created all of the various nations, even though he could have created just one nation, so that we might get to know one another.[130] My friend Sara says that this is a gift from God to us, to be created in such diversity that we must learn from one another. She told me that this is precisely why she thinks that engaging in dialogical friendships is incumbent upon her as a Muslim. Coupled with this foundational belief is the example of the Prophet Muhammad.

---

[130] Qur'an 49:13.

There is a story of the Prophet hosting a Christian delegation in Medina. The Muslims and Christians had a heated debate on the differences between their respective traditions. At one point, the Christians asked for the Prophet's protection so they could leave the city and perform their prayers. The Prophet surprised them by inviting them into his mosque to pray, saying that just because their traditions had differences did not mean that they should not respect and show hospitality to the others' practices.[131]

This tradition is vitally important to helping Muslims create a theological framework for engaging in dialogical friendships across lines of difference. It seems that there is a robust framework within Islam that gives purpose to the act of being friends with both Christians and Jews.

From a Jewish perspective, there is again a scriptural precedent for reciprocal relationships to be found in the understanding that all humans are bearers of the divine image. "When engaged in a conversation with a person of different religious commitment I discover we disagree in matters sacred to us, does the image of God I face disappear?"[132] This is a fantastic question that deserves some reflection. How often are we quick to demonize the other because of a disagreement about theology? This question, posed by a rabbi, has an implied answer in the negative. The image of God in everyone is part of the framework for Jews when it comes to engaging in relationships with religious others. In the Talmud, the Jewish book of

---

[131] Patel, *Sacred Ground*, 149.
[132] Heschel, *No Religion Is an Island*, 123.

civil and ceremonial law, we find this: "For this reason was man created single (whereas of every other species many were created)...that there should be peace among human beings: one cannot say to his neighbor, my ancestor was nobler than thine (Talmud, Sanhedrin, 37a)."[133] It is easy to see the echo of this teaching in the Muslim belief that God created us so that we would get to know one another. Coupled with these concepts, there are the stories of Elisha and Naaman; Ruth, Naomi, and Boaz; Rahab the prostitute; and Daniel and Nebuchadnezzar, among others, to demonstrate that the very preservation of the Jewish people relied heavily upon a theology of reciprocal relationships across lines of difference.

Life Changing and Life Giving

The Harvard Pluralism Project's Diana Eck has a clear and concise way of explaining this concept of the life-changing, life-giving nature of dialogical friendships. Noting that diversity alone is simply a cultural fact, she states that, "Mere diversity without real encounter and relationship will yield increasing tensions in our societies."[134] So, the first point is that pluralism, or in our case dialogical friendship, is the "energetic engagement with diversity."[135] I have heard Eboo Patel say that diversity isn't a virtue to be praised in and of itself. In that speech to students at Monmouth College, he

---

[133] Ibid.
[134] "What Is Pluralism?" The Pluralism Project, accessed September 24, 2015, http://www.pluralism.org/pluralism/what_is_pluralism.
[135] Ibid.

noted that diversity could lead to increased divisions and isolation, as well as increased tension and ultimately violence.[136] We saw this reality play out in situations such as the ones in Ferguson, Missouri, and Baltimore, Maryland, in 2014. Both of these communities were incredibly diverse. However that diversity led to disengagement between whites and blacks, rather than an energetic engagement. Because of this diverse disengagement, isolation turned to violence when racial tensions intensified to a breaking point. *To engage energetically with diversity is to give life to a situation nearing death.* Not sitting back and letting history take its course, instead a dialogical friend chooses to give life by seeking to understand the perspective of the other for the sake of peace.

Secondly, a dialogical friendship is active in its search for understanding across lines of religious difference. Passivity looks like searching the Internet for answers related to questions we have about other religions. My friend Gil asked me once if I would defend sharia law, given that it allows for forced conversions, stonings, and executions if someone becomes apostate or leaves the Islamic faith. He later admitted that his sources for understanding sharia law come from a few websites that he has read, which are looking at sharia from a non-Muslim perspective. I told him that the best way he could find real answers for how American Muslims understand sharia law is to become friends with them and ask them about it. Activity looks

---

[136] This is from a speech given by Eboo Patel at Monmouth College on October 30, 2014. I was in attendance.

like engaging in dialogical friendships with people who believe much differently than we do. This means that dialogical friendships take some effort. If we are choosing to engage with the diversity around us, then this next step involves choosing to ask real questions with the goal of finding a path to understanding.

"The problem to be faced is: how to combine loyalty to one's own tradition with reverence for different traditions?"[137] Perhaps the most important point made by Eck is this: "[Pluralism] is not relativism, but *the encounter of commitments*...It means holding our deepest differences, even our religious differences, not in isolation, but in relationship to one another."[138] This is important for several reasons. First, many people equate pluralism with relativism. If we are to embrace pluralism, many people believe we will have to lay aside our own commitments to what we believe in order to get along. Rather boldly, Diana Eck proposes that pluralism (and I would add dialogical friendships) helps us to *clarify what it is that we are actually committed to*.

I was talking with my friend Bassel recently, and he told me that the challenging questions that he receives through his work with Eid.Pray.Love cause him to find reasons for why he believes the things that he does as a Muslim. When someone asks a question that he doesn't have an answer to, he is forced to find an answer and therefore clarify what it is that he actually believes. My friend Seher,

---

[137] Heschel, *No Religion Is an Island*, 126.
[138] Ibid.

also a Muslim, told me that her relationship with her best friend, David (a Christian), has made her into a better Muslim and him into a better Christian.[139] How has this happened? For one, Seher has seen that her belief in the holy books (the Torah, the Psalms, the Gospels, and the Qur'an) is simply worthless if she hasn't read them herself. Instead of being comfortable with that fact, she has, through her friendship with David, been given the impetus to read the Bible—the Jewish and Christian scriptures. In so doing, she has discovered new commitments that she didn't have before as a Muslim that have changed the way she looks at faith, as well as the way she looks at Judaism and Christianity. Here we see the life-changing and life-giving nature of dialogical friendships.

The final point from Eck regarding pluralism is also quite relevant to our understanding of the meaning and purpose of engaging in dialogical friendships.

> Fourth, pluralism is *based on dialogue*. The language of pluralism is that of dialogue and encounter, give and take, criticism and self-criticism. Dialogue means both speaking and listening, and that process reveals both common understandings and real differences. Dialogue does not mean everyone at the "table" will agree with one another. Pluralism involves the commitment to being at the table—with one's commitments.[140]

A dialogical friendship requires two commitments: to the friendship

---

[139] You can listen to these and more conversations on the Frienemies podcast at http://www.frienemies.podbean.com.
[140] The Pluralism Project, "What Is Pluralism?"

itself and to one's own religious commitments. I imagine a dialogical friendship looking like a religious potluck. Each friend brings something unique and delicious to the table. We fill our plate with each and every food that looks good. Some of the food is new to us, and some is familiar. Some of it tastes so good we want to get more. Other food isn't worth eating ever again. As we learn from one another or taste the food that is brought to the table by our friend, we receive two invitations as we taste and see. The first invitation is to pick up something that we hear that is good and true or worth tasting over and over again—that would be to pick up a new commitment. The other invitation is to acknowledge that something we brought to the potluck really isn't worth tasting anymore—that would be to lay down a negative commitment.

The second conversation I had with Jamal occurred one week after the first, prior to the start of classes at the English center one evening. He had taken my Bible in order to read it on the night of our first conversation, and he had read all of the first three Gospels—Matthew, Mark, and Luke—in a week's time. Although the Bible is not readily available in Jordan, it is also a holy book of Islam, so Jamal wasn't doing anything wrong by reading it. He told me he had a question because of his reading. "Why does Jesus call himself the 'Son of Man' all of the time?" Suddenly I realized that I truly had no idea. I had gone to Bible college, and I had been a youth pastor, but I had no answer for Jamal on this one. The only explanation I had been given growing up was that Jesus was called the Son of God and the

Son of Man, indicating that he was fully God and fully man. It's not a good explanation and not even a true reading of the text.

All of these thoughts were running through my head as I muttered, "I don't have a good answer for you." I realized what I had been given, what I had been at least marginally committed to, was not worth carrying around anymore. My understanding of the "Son of Man" was insufficient. I needed to find answers and clarify my commitments. And I did. The only reason this happened was because Jamal and I engaged in a dialogical friendship that challenged each of us to decide what beliefs we held that were worthless, either about God or each other, and to take up new commitments in the process.

I once heard author Peter Rollins explain that true dialogue is not meant to change the other person into looking, thinking, or acting in the same way that one does. Rather, dialogue is a means to becoming a better version of oneself. He used this example: If Republicans and Democrats engage in a dialogue, a true dialogue, the purpose cannot be for all the Republicans to become Democrats or for all Democrats to become Republicans. That's what monologue does. Rather, it is an invitation to see oneself through the eyes of the other, in order to become a better Republican or a better Democrat.[141] A dialogical friendship is not a friendship based on outcomes or end games but is simply based upon coming to an understanding of one another. Imagine, just for a second, what the world would look like if

---

[141] Peter Rollins spent some time hanging out with the people at our church in early 2015.

Christians truly understood Muslims and Jews, if Jews truly understood Muslims and Christians, and if Muslims truly understood Christians and Jews. Through that understanding, I am convinced we will create spaces for peace to break out as allies and true friends of the other.

Postlude

A contest for drawing cartoons of the Prophet Muhammad in Garland, Texas; a biker protest (with cartoons) in Phoenix, Arizona; an anti-Ramadan biker barbeque in Colorado on the first day of Ramadan 2015; anti-Islam advertisements on buses in major cities; and the shooting of three Muslims in North Carolina, coupled with a massacre on a beach in Tunisia, a suicide bomb in a mosque in Kuwait (not to mention those that occurred in Saudi Arabia and Yemen), a beheaded boss in France, 3.5 million refugees from Syria, and ISIS, created an important moment for Muslims in America in 2015.

"We need to make an effort to become part of the mainstream culture, so people can see that we are just human beings like them." A fiery, passionate Muslim woman spoke those words to the leadership of her mosque as she insisted that they needed to participate in SE7EN FAST by hosting a SE7EN FEAST at their mosque that year. She was bold. She was unapologetic. She believed that creating opportunities for Christians and Jews to engage with Muslims in our community mattered immensely, especially given the world situation and the situation in our own country at the time. She wanted the youth of her Muslim community to have hope that things can be better than they currently are. She and her husband even went so far as to foot the bill for food, no matter the cost, so that as many non-Muslims as possible would have the opportunity to engage in conversation and break bread with Muslims on July 7, 2015.

Despite all of the stereotypes one might have about women in Islam—that they are to remain silent, that they are oppressed, that they are powerless—she blew all of those stereotypes apart. She spoke her mind without fear in the presence of two other male members of the mosque. She was heard. She had a voice. She wasn't told to know her place or to keep silent. Indeed, she couldn't keep silent.

And neither should we. I also believe that the first step toward changing our own fear into love for our neighbors, strangers, and enemies is to get face-to-face, to hear and be heard, to know and be known by them. If we have any hope of believing a different story about one another, we must make the effort to engage in loving relationships with the other.

As the world continues to break apart all around us, the question is whether we believe that another way is possible. We can no longer "live and let live." That philosophy of life is passive, disengaged, and potentially dangerous. If we don't have any relationships with people who are different from us, we don't have any way of seeing and being hope in our communities. If we don't have any dialogical friendships across lines of religious difference, we have no chance of our love transforming strangers and enemies into neighbors. Individualism and isolation are enemies of peace. We all need to fight our impulse to hunker down, to ignore, and to keep our distance.

If you get the chance to change your story, then change your story. I hope that you will see that relating across lines of difference doesn't require you to believe or be any less than what you are. All it requires is openness, openness to the perspective of someone else to help form you into a better version of yourself. That's what dialogical friendships are all about. Pursue this, and you pursue peace. If you don't know where to start, keep reading.

Afterword
Putting It into Practice

Love expands with use.

—David Brooks[142]

[142] "David Brooks to Grads: Be Really Good at Making Commitments," *Time*, last modified June 16, 2015, accessed September 29, 2015, http://www.time.com/3922993/david-brooks-graduation-speech-dartmouth.

Risking Nothing and Everything All at Once

In this book, I have done my best to provide a reason for Jews, Christians, and Muslims to engage in dialogical friendships with one another. You may be thinking at this point, "OK, I get it. But I don't have any friends who are of a different faith. This all sounds good, but I don't have any idea how or where to make this happen for myself." My friend Autumn, a Christian, once told me that there are many Muslim moms at the school when she picks up her kids. She said she has often wanted to say hello, but they always seem to avoid eye contact and often seem unapproachable. She said they seem as if they aren't interested in conversation. So, she hasn't ever said hello.

This is a challenge on multiple levels. One challenge is for American Muslims to step outside of their comfort zones and open themselves up to being known by their neighbors, strangers, and enemies. Mehdi Hasan, host of Al Jazeera's *Up Front*, told a gathering of about five hundred Muslims that the fact that two-thirds of Americans don't know a Muslim is a Muslim issue. He told the audience that it is their responsibility to step out of their comfort zones and to engage in relationships. When I heard this, I thought back to another conversation with a Muslim man in my community. One evening, while my wife was working at the Islamic school, she was invited to come to a big cookout, celebrating the groundbreaking for the new mosque to be built behind the school. We went and took our friends Zach and Elise with us. There were hundreds of people from the Muslim community at this event—and we were the four non-Muslims. As Zach and I stood in line for food, no one was talking to us. We got plenty of curious stares but no conversation.

Not willing to go through this experience without meeting someone, I turned to the man ahead of me in line and introduced myself. I asked him what he did for a living, and he told me that he was a doctor at one of our local hospitals. Then, naturally, he asked me what I did. I told him that I worked with Christians, teaching them about Islam and how to build bridges with Muslims. He responded, "Wow. Thank you. I need to be doing that." Precisely. He went on to say that he had lived in America for ten years and had never talked with anyone about what he believed. I encouraged him to do so, since I am convinced that the greatest barrier between Christians and Muslims is a lack of knowledge, which leads to fear and isolation. We need Muslims to open themselves up to being known and to share with others about what they believe if we have any hope that things will change.

Another challenge is for American Christians and American Jews to step out of their comfort zones and also open up to engaging in conversations with Muslims in our midst. Earlier I shared a story of my wife saying hello to a woman at the grocery store. Although this seems simplistic, I believe it truly is a transformative act. As more non-Muslims continue to extend welcome and kindness to Muslims, I believe that the imagined social and cultural barrier between us will begin to dissipate. When Autumn told me about her apprehension to meet the Muslim moms at her kids' school, I told her that she should just take a risk and ignore the impulse to keep the status quo. If we feel like we should do or say something out of love for our neighbors, strangers, or enemies, we need to act on it. The status remains quo because too many of us choose isolation over engagement. We need to change that.

Purposeful Engagement

I acknowledge that most people aren't just going to say hello to strangers. We have been socially conditioned otherwise. Coupled with that is the reality that these random interactions won't typically lead to long-term dialogical friendships. We need some more purposeful ways of meeting people if we hope to establish new friendships and make the peace that we all hope for become a possibility. With that in mind, here are some ways that others have connected across lines of religious difference that might inspire some new ideas for you as you seek to be a person of faith who is also seeking to make peace through dialogical friendships.

On almost every college and university campus, there are religious student groups, such as Hillel House (a Jewish student organization), the Muslim Students Association, and various Christian organizations (Cru, InterVarsity, Chi Alpha, and so on). Hillel Houses and MSAs regularly sponsor events on campus for non-Jews and non-Muslims to learn about their respective faiths. Christian groups, admittedly, sponsor these types of events less frequently (and those events are often geared solely toward trying to convert non-Christians). Go to these events and meet people. It's as simple as that.

My friend Trish runs a student organization for international students in rural Missouri. At the beginning of every year, they have a goat roast to gather students together from all religious backgrounds to break bread together. This event, and her organization as a whole, provides spaces for people to develop dialogical friendships. One year, a local mosque was set ablaze by an anti-Muslim arsonist. One Christian student decided that the Christian community needed to express publicly that they were standing in solidarity with Muslims. She organized a fundraiser for the Muslim community to help repair the building but also to create an opportunity for Muslims and Christians to meet one another. Hundreds of people gathered together in solidarity with the Muslim community at the event, and it went a long way toward making peace between Christians and Muslims. A women's group of Christians and Muslims was even birthed out of it.

Organizations such as these exist on many of our local campuses. International students need help in many ways adjusting to life in America. Some groups provide free transport from the airport. Others provide help in purchasing furniture and finding housing. There are groups that provide language partners for English language learners. Others simply provide help in learning how to drive and helping these students get driver's licenses. All it takes is for you to find out what is going on to help international students on your campus and to find out how you might get involved.

If you live in a city with a mosque, a synagogue, or a church, this is even easier. Muslims gather for prayer on Fridays at the mosque, and many mosques have Sunday School on Sundays. Contact your local mosque to schedule a time to go, and when you do, meet people there. If there is a synagogue, you could go to a Shabbat service. If there is a church, you could go to a service on a Sunday morning. Don't just go alone. Take a friend with you to share in the experience. No doubt there will be many questions that arise just from observing the service, and these questions are a perfect starting point for conversation and potential friendship with the *other*.

The Foundation for Ethnic Understanding sponsors what they call "The Season of Twinning."

> Mosques and synagogues, Muslim and Jewish student groups, young leadership bodies and women's organizations "twin" with each other in cities around the world and hold encounters focused on celebrating commonalities in our two faith traditions, standing together against Islamophobia and anti-Semitism and performing acts of social service together in recognition of the common moral imperative in both Islam and Judaism to help those most in need.[143]

The purpose, beyond a public display of solidarity and cooperation, is for "Jews and Muslims around the world to meet, learn from each

---

[143] "The Weekend of Twinning," *Foundation for Ethnic Understanding*, accessed on September 29, 2015, http://ffeu.org/twinning.html.

other and to form personal friendships."[144] Their website provides information on when and where events are taking place in various cities across the United States and even throughout the world. Often, events such as these provide a reason for people of different faiths to come together in order to learn from one another and to work together to make peace in our communities.

Peace Catalyst is another organization whose sole purpose is to work toward Muslim-Christian understanding. They accomplish this through various events, two of which are Peace Feasts and Jesus Dialogues. A Peace Feast is a celebration of God, food, and diversity. The concept is simple: bring food and eat said food together. There is nothing more powerful than eating delicious food across the table from someone of a different religious background and discovering his or her culture and story.

> Jesus is a significant person in both Christianity and Islam. Jesus is known for his teaching of peace and the blessing of being a peacemaker. There is great ignorance and misunderstanding about the beliefs and teachings of Jesus from both faith traditions. We want to encourage churches and mosques to begin open and honest dialogue about Jesus from the perspectives of both faiths.[145]

What a Jesus Dialogue is, then, is a forum for Christians and Muslims to hear from each other's religious leaders about who Jesus

---

[144] Ibid.

[145] "Jesus Dialogues," Peace Catalyst International, accessed on September 29, 2015, http://www.peace-catalyst.net/programs/jesus-dialogues.

is to them. Beyond just hearing, when Christians and Muslims gather together for a single purpose, dialogical friendships are right around the corner. The gift that Peace Catalyst gives to every community is its openness to help anyone set up and promote these events.

SE7EN FAST is another grassroots, event-based opportunity for engagement across lines of difference. SE7EN FAST invites non-Muslims to fast on the same day during Ramadan, to give what would have been spent on food to an organization that helps provide food to people in war-torn countries, and then to break fast with Muslims in their community (called a SE7EN FEAST). "This event will foster new relationships between people who share many beliefs and also share the communities in which they live, allowing opportunities for people to find ways to engage in meaningful, life-changing and life-giving relationships with people they don't know, understand, and may be afraid of."[146] SE7EN FAST is an easy way to connect Christians, Jews, and Muslims in a given community and potentially help them begin dialogical friendships as a result.

It's Up to You

There are many more organizations and opportunities that exist in places all around our country for Muslims, Christians, and Jews to get into the same room and let the fear and isolation melt away. I have shared these with you in order to encourage you to put into

---

[146] "About Us," SE7EN FAST, accessed on September 29, 2015, http://www.se7enfast.com/about. If the language sounds familiar, it's because I wrote it.

practice what we have been talking about throughout this book—namely to make neighbors out of strangers and enemies through dialogical friendships across lines of religious difference. You have the power to change the narrative of fear and isolation in your community. You have the power to make peace a reality in your community and in our world. If that peace is possible, it starts with individuals. It starts with you.

May our faith guide us on pathways of peace as we participate in being the blessing in the world that we have been called into as children of Abraham. That blessing is ours to receive and ours to share.

[God], make us instruments of your peace.
Where there is hatred, let us sow love;
Where there is injury, pardon;
Where there is discord, union;
Where there is doubt, faith;
Where there is despair, hope;
Where there is darkness, light;
Where there is sadness, joy.
Grant that we may not so much seek to be consoled as to console;
To be understood as to understand;
To be loved as to love.
For it is in giving that we receive;
It is in pardoning that we are pardoned;
And it is in dying that we are born to eternal life.
Amen.[147]

---

[147] "A Prayer Attributed to St. Francis," *Episcopal Book of Common Prayer*, 833.

J ROBERT EAGAN

Bibliography

Books and Journal Articles

Aslan, Reza. *No God but God: The Origins, Evolution, and Future of Islam*. New York: Random House, 2006.

Balentine, Samuel E. *Leviticus: Interpretation*. Louisville: John Knox Press, 2002.

Balentine, Samuel E. *Prayer in the Hebrew Bible: The Drama of Divine-Human Dialogue*. Minneapolis: Fortress Press, 1993.

Briggs, Richard S., and Joel N. Lohr, eds. *A Theological Introduction to the Pentateuch: Interpreting the Torah as Christian Scripture*. Grand Rapids: Baker Academic, 2012.

Brueggemann, Walter. *Praying the Psalms*. Eugene: Wipf and Stock Publishing, 2007.

Camp, Lee. *Who Is My Enemy? Questions American Christians Must Face about Islam—and Themselves*. Grand Rapids: Brazos Press, 2011.

Clark, Kelly James, ed. *Abraham's Children: Liberty and Tolerance in an Age of Religious Conflict*. New Haven: Yale University Press, 2012.

Cole, Darrell. *When God Says War Is Right: The Christian Perspective on When and How to Fight*. Colorado Springs: Waterbrook Press, 2002.

Coope, Jessica A. "Religious and Cultural Conversion to Islam in Ninth-Century Umayyad Cordoba." *Journal of World History* 4, no. 1 (Spring 1993): 47–68.

Davis, Nancy J., and Robert V. Robinson. "Overcoming Movement Obstacles by the Religiously Orthodox: The Muslim Brotherhood in Egypt, the Shas in Israel, Comunione e Liberazione in Italy, and the Salvation Army in the United States." *American Journal of Sociology* 114, no. 5 (March 2009): 1302–1349.

Fatah, Tarek. *The Jew Is Not My Enemy: Unveiling the Myths that Fuel Muslim Anti-Semitism*. Toronto: McLelland & Stewart Ltd., 2010.

Hart, Michael. *The 100: A Ranking of the Most Influential Persons in History*. New York: Citadel, 1978.

Heschel, Abraham Joshua. "No Religion Is an Island." *Union Seminary Quarterly Review* 21 no. 2, 1 (January 1966): 117–134.

McLaren, Brian D. *Why Did Jesus, Moses, the Buddha, and Mohammed Cross the Road? Christian Identity in a Multi-Faith World.* New York: Jericho Books, 2012.

Meier, John P. "The Historical Jesus and the Historical Samaritans: What Can Be Said?" *Biblica* 81, no. 2 (2000): 563–573.

Milgrom, Jacob D. *Leviticus: A Book of Ritual and Ethics.* Minneapolis: Fortress Press, 2004.

Neudecker, Reinhard. "'And You Shall Love Your Neighbor as Yourself—I Am the Lord' (Lev. 19, 18) in Jewish Interpretation." *Biblica* 73, no. 4 (1992): 496–517.

Ogletree, Thomas W. "The Essential Unity of the Love Commands: Moving Beyond Paradox." *The Journal of Religious Ethics* 34, no. 4 (Dec. 2007): 695–700.

Patel, Eboo. *Sacred Ground: Pluralism, Prejudice, and the Promise of America.* Boston: Beacon Press, 2012.

Stassen, Glen H., and David P. Gushee. *Kingdom Ethics: Following Jesus in Contemporary Context.* Downers Grove, MI: IVP Academic, 2003.

Volf, Miroslav, Ghazi bin Muhammad, and Melissa Yarrington, eds. *A Common Word: Muslims and Christians on Loving God and Neighbor.* Grand Rapids: William B. Eerdmans Pub. Co., 2010.

Yoder, John Howard. *The Original Revolution: Essays on Christian Pacifism.* Scottdale: Herald Press, 1971.

Websites

Al Jazeera English. "Magazine: Meet Israel's boycotters." Last modified June 8, 2015. Accessed September 29, 2015. http://www.aljazeera.com/indepth/features/2015/05/magazine-meet-israel-boycotters-150528072013581.html.

Foundation for Ethnic Understanding. "The Weekend of Twinning." About. Accessed on September 29, 2015. http://ffeu.org/twinning.html.

The *Guardian*. "Catholic Church in Israel Badly Damaged by Suspected Arson Attack." Last modified June 18, 2015. Accessed June 29, 2015. http://www.theguardian.com/world/2015/jun/18/catholic-church-multiplication-israel-damaged-possible-arson-attack.

The *Independent*. "'I Don't Have a Single American Friend': Photo Essay Titled 'Will Box for Passport' Reveals Profile of Boston Bombing Suspect Tamerlan Tsarnaev." Last modified April 19, 2013. Accessed July 7, 2015. http://www.independent.co.uk/news/world/americas/i-dont-have-a-single-american-friend-photo-essay-titled-will-box-for-passport-reveals-profile-of-boston-bombing-suspect-tamerlan-tsarnaev-8580575.html.

Martin Luther King Jr. and the Global Freedom Struggle. "Loving Your Enemies, Sermon Delivered at Dexter Avenue Baptist Church." Accessed on September 24, 2015. http://kingencyclopedia.stanford.edu/encyclopedia/documentsentry/doc_loving_your_enemies/.

Peace Catalyst International. "Jesus Dialogues." Accessed on September 29, 2015. http://www.peace-catalyst.net/programs/jesus-dialogues.

The Pluralism Project. "What Is Pluralism?" Accessed September 24, 2015. http://www.pluralism.org/pluralism/what_is_pluralism.

Poetry. "No Man Is an Island." Accessed September 29, 2015. https://web.cs.dal.ca/~johnston/poetry/island.html.

Pop Chassid. "10 Images of Jewish-Muslim Unity that Go Beyond the Headlines." Last modified February 17, 2015. Accessed July 2, 2015. http://popchassid.com/10-photos-muslim-jewish-unity/.

SE7EN FAST. "About Us." Accessed on September 29, 2015. http://www.se7enfast.com/about.

Time. "David Brooks to Grads: Be Really Good at Making Commitments." Last modified June 16, 2015. Accessed September 29, 2015. http://www.time.com/3922993/david-brooks-graduation-speech-dartmouth.

Time. "Transcript: Read the Speech Pope Francis Gave to Congress." Last modified on September 24, 2015. Accessed on September 27, 2015. http://time.com/4048176/pope-francis-us-visit-congress-transcript.

UNHCR. "Figures at a Glance." Accessed January 21, 2016.

http://www.unhcr.org/pages/49c3646c11.html.

USA Today. "Charleston Victims Wield Power of Forgiveness: Column." Last modified June 22, 2015. Accessed July 23, 2015. http://www.usatoday.com/story/opinion/2015/06/21/charleston-church-shooting-families-forgiveness-column/29069731.

The United States Conference of Catholic Bishops. "Solidarity." Accessed July 23, 2015. http://www.usccb.org/beliefs-and-teachings/what-we-believe/catholic-social-teaching/solidarity.cfm.

About the Author

J. Robert Eagan (MA in Theology and Ministry, Fuller Theological
Seminary) is a teacher, writer, and activator with the Isaac Ishmael
Initiative. He is the cofounder of SE7EN FAST, a national event
designed to get non-Muslims and Muslims in the same room to break
bread together in the name of peace. *Of Strangers & Enemies* is his first
book. He lives with his wife, Jessey, and two kids, Obi and Guinevere, in
Lakewood, Colorado. Learn more at jroberteagan.com or follow him on
Twitter: @Se7enFast.